BECOMING THE PRESENCE OF GOD

Michael Ford

BECOMING THE PRESENCE OF GOD

Contemplative Ministry for Everybody

the columba press

First published in 2016 by

the columba press

55A Spruce Avenue,
Stillorgan Industrial Park,
Blackrock, Co. Dublin

Cover image and design by Helene Pertl I The Columba Press
Origination by The Columba Press
Printed by ScandBook AB, Sweden

ISBN 978 1 78218 234 4

The author and publishers are grateful to Sister Jean-Marie Howe
OCSO for permission to quote extensively from her writings which
were published as *Spiritual Journey: The Monastic Way*, 1989, St Bede's
Publications, Petersham, Massachusetts, and *Secret of the Heart:
Spiritual Being*, 2005, Cistercian Publications, Kalamazoo, Michigan.

For Robert Durback,
who inspired the text

~

With love and gratitude to
my mother, Margaret, and brother, Nigel,
who support me unfailingly

~

For Chris, Lee, Mark and Myles,
whose priestly stories lie within

We exist solely for this:
to be the place
   God has chosen
for His presence,
   His manifestation
in the world,
   His epiphany.

Thomas Merton

Gratitudes

I am immensely grateful to Sister Jean-Marie Howe OCSO and Sister Kathleen Waters OCSO, of the Trappistine Abbey of Notre-Dame de l'Assomption in Rogersville, New Brunswick, Canada, and to Mother Paula Fairlie OSB and the community of Curzon Park Abbey, Chester, England. For their assistance with this project over the past five years and supportive friendship during it, my appreciation also to Alex Barrow, Lesley Bilinda, Alastair Blaine, Tom and Jessica Birch, Philip Butcher, Sheila Cook, David Cowie, Jack Crawshaw, Thelma Cridge, Jessie Daniels White, Andrew Down, Geoff Dumbreck and Oliver Coates, Geoff Driver, Richard Edwards, Barnaby and Bella Ford, Ann Fulton, Jack Good, Eva Heymann, Jean Hole, Christopher and Laura Johnson, Christopher and Carolyn Landau, John Lee, Alison and Malcolm Mathew, Sheena McMain, Sam and Jenny McNally-Cross, RoseMary Murphy, Myles Ronald Owen, Janet Paynter, Phil Pegum, Luke Penkett, Chris Pickles, Dee and Pietro Pizzo, Laurence and Caz Powell, James Proctor, Anthony Redmond, Martha Reeves, Alex Rogers, John and Sheila Roles, Lee Taylor and Fabiano Silva, Michael Smith, Justine Sturman, Raymond and Rose Tomkinson, David Torevell, Simon Vivian, Dara Westby, Mark Woodrow, Josh and Emma Young. Special gratitude to the late Suzanne Leighton. My thanks also to Patrick O'Donoghue, Leeann Gallagher, Lisa Keating, Helene Pertl, Shane McCoy, Ellen Monnelly and all at The Columba Press for their professionalism and support.

Contents

Introducing ...
The Monk and The Postman

This is a book to encourage you to claim your vocation to be a contemplative in the world. You might be a practising believer or you might remain on the fringes of institutional religion because you feel you do not have a strong enough faith or because your personal situation in life alienates you from the church. On the other hand, you might have been ordained or have made a monastic profession but are still yearning to come closer to God in order to serve others well. Know you are welcome on this journey.

The premise of the text is simple but challenging to live out: we are each called, in our uniqueness, not just to represent, but to *become* the divine presence for others. But I believe we can only do this authentically if our hearts are rooted in the silence of interior prayer. It is a ministry for everyone, ordained and not ordained, professed or not professed, but it demands that we follow in the footsteps of the humble, self-effacing Christ rather than mount the ladder of self-serving ambition. There is a chasm between the two approaches: one is 'contemplative', the other 'clerical'.

These insights emerged when I was working as a staff journalist for the BBC and struck up a transatlantic correspondence with a man who had spent many years on his knees as a faithful Trappist monk at an abbey in South Carolina. Then, one day, he left the cloisters and ended up on his feet – as a postman.

In his letters, as well as articles, Robert Durback described his joy as a contemplative in the world where he had created his own unique ministry on the doorstep of other people's lives. We corresponded for several years, eventually meeting in Canada. Every few months he would send immaculately typed dispatches or neatly written notes on beige-coloured cards. Each would feature an element of creation he had captured on camera – a sunset, a landscape or a flower in close-up. Bob became a soul friend during that short time, unveiling for me the secrets of authentic spiritual living. I kept the correspondence in a plastic wallet and stored it in the attic.

Then one day, twenty years later, at a low point in my life, I happened to come across those letters again. I was feeling disillusioned with religion that morning as I stumbled across this stash of spiritual gold. As I crouched beneath the eaves, I began studying the old monastic correspondence like a jeweller uncovering a precious topaz.

There, in the stillness of the loft, I found myself undergoing not so much a reconversion but more a re-enlightenment. As my one-time monastic correspondent reminded me, living a spiritual life was not so much a matter of saying prayers as cultivating a relationship with God, something I had known all along but which seemed to have been shrouded since ordination as a deacon a year or so before.

I had soon realised that I would never be at home as an official representative of a particular branch of the institutional church. It just wasn't my world. I found it religious but not all that spiritual, infantilising rather than dignifying. While I met some really fine priests, I also ran into some unnerving and dysfunctional behaviour which I had already discovered (more distantly) as a journalist. It was clear to me that it did not arise from a contemplative spirit. There were occasions when envy and resentment towered over compassion and humanity. I felt alienated and alone; and I could identify with the mocked, abandoned Christ. Tainted by experience, perhaps, I found myself estranged and contained, although the parishioners I met in different contexts were extremely supportive and continue to be. Furthermore, after being made a deacon, I couldn't pray naturally and my sense of self seemed to disintegrate. Unable to embrace the contemplative life formed in me over many years, I became profoundly unhappy and kept recalling the words of a Desert Father (Abba Poemen) who implored us not to give our hearts to that which fails to satisfy them. I knew I had to leave.

Admittedly, though, I was different – and not only because I was marked out as a journalist. Prompted by the ecumenical spirit of Brother Roger of Taizé, I had lived for much of my adult life in both the Anglican and Roman Catholic traditions – and knew I needed both. I could particularly relate to the Benedictine monk who said: 'I stand in the Christian tradition, its catholic form, which I would spell with a small *c*. *Catholic* means "all-embracing".'[1] And professionally, as a religious broadcaster and writer, my constituency had no bounds.

After many long conversations and much prayer, spiritual guides intuited that my deeper vocation was to be a bridge between denominations and urged me to claim my uniqueness as a free spirit without having to justify it. They believed this contemplative calling would have to be lived out on the margins of institutional religion or I would lose my truth forever, as one of them put it.

Unshackled from the institution, I now feel I can minister again across the denominational divide. This, I sense, is more in keeping with my true spiritual calling as my ecumenical work continues on and off the airwaves. Every week a new person is in touch, sometimes in crisis or perhaps looking for direction and support at a painful time. There are retreats to give, programmes to prepare and funerals to take, as requested. It has become a ministry on the margins with my website (hermitagewithin.co.uk) holding it all together. I feel at peace again now.

Mine, though, is not an isolated story by any means, even among those I trained with. The first few years of parish life have long been described as 'trial by curacy' – and not without good reason. While some curates thrive in their first positions, others do not because the vicar–curate relationship is not always a healthy one. I have spoken to many priests through the years about their experiences of curacy. From them I have learned that insecure training incumbents can become pathologically envious of their curates' gifts and jealous of their popularity with parishioners. A number of them have apparently lied about their curates to bishops, either to protect themselves or to get back at their charges. Some curates have had to move to other parishes and dioceses, or left ministry altogether to follow completely different walks of life.

Of course there are many professional and caring parish priests, who train their curates competently, but a significant proportion is clearly short of the mark and would never be tolerated by any other institution. The power and control dynamic that the (generally more immature and scheming) vicar tries to wield over the (often more creative and psychologically integrated) curate is at best neurotic and at worst abusive, leaving no small number of newly ordained deacons and priests feeling disillusioned and betrayed by the church they have served all their lives. They swiftly realise that institutional ministry does not always follow in the footsteps of the poor man of Nazareth. Some even wonder, not how these men and women became trainers, but how they ever managed to get ordained in the first place.

The genuinely prayerful and unambitious priest will invariably prove to be the most effective training incumbent. The more suspicious and fearful vicar, a product of the prevailing ecclesiastical culture, will inevitably seek to dominate and undermine someone he or she perceives as a threat. This type of bully usually turns out to be a gossip as well.

The difficulty ordained people tend to experience with the institutional church is that it puts the procedural before the personal. Yet Jesus Christ, in whose name it officiates, worked on entirely the opposite principle. Some clergy have been badly bruised because of a nervous hierarchical tendency to become legalistic and distanced when problems arise, instead of offering what the church is supposed to be noted for – relational pastoral care. Officials who are concerned more with neurotic control than loving-kindness make a mockery of the faith they purportedly espouse.

So, as I was packing away my cassocks and stoles in the attic that day, the former monk's words inaugurated a process of reconnecting me with the person I had been and which conventional ordained life had strangely occluded. With a beguiling elegance, they drew attention to the two movements of prayer which could be expressed in different ways: a growing awareness of the presence of God and then, at a given point, a response to that awareness. 'For instance,' Bob explained, 'a walk in the woods may give me a sharper awareness of my connectedness to all living things. When I get home, I might feel a strong urge to open the scriptures to keep this sense of connectedness alive. Or I might be moved to pick up the phone or write a letter to someone who's had a death in the family or who is going through a difficult time. The rhythm is there in either instance: awareness/response. It just expresses itself in different ways.'

Bob believed regular spiritual reading (*lectio divina*) provided 'grist for the mill' of a person's life. I had valued this practice over many years but, as soon as I had been ordained, it had seemed to lose significance. I fed off my correspondent's words like a ravenous crow: 'Both spiritual and non-spiritual writings can till the necessary inner predisposition to awareness, as can classical music as it cultivates an interior sensitivity to beauty. As one maps out one's spiritual terrain, it is essential to make choices and decisions about one's lifestyle so that one's relationship with God grows in the process.'

The more I familiarised myself with Bob's journey, the more I came to realise that, like him, my real vocation was to be a contemplative in the world and minister from there. When Bob decided to leave the safe and structured world of monastic living after thirteen years, he was immediately confronted with decisions about how he could stay in touch with all the things that had been important to him there. Having chosen to continue a celibate lifestyle, he had to devise practical ways of helping to deepen a prayerful relationship with God. He was living with his mother, so he arranged to rebuild part of her basement in order to have a place to be alone. 'It was too much of a shock to come from the absolute silence of a Trappist monastery to the mainstream life, so I made myself a place for silence and prayer – and I spent plenty of time in it,' he wrote.

'It started me off on the right foot. After my mother died, I bought a home of my own, a small brick house in the suburbs. I took one bedroom, cleared it of everything and made it into an empty space with a chair, a side table for my books, a big crucifix and a candle. One of my favourite positions for prayer, which I learned in the monastery, is lying flat on my face. I like that position because it is a way of making a statement with the whole of my body.'

Delivering mail on Route 4016 out of a branch post office meant an early start, a discipline for which Bob had more than adequate formation. He would roll out of bed at a quarter to five and begin the day with a personal prayer formulated long ago. He gave thanks for the gift of another day, asking that he might have the grace to live it in the freedom and joy 'that is the gift of the indwelling Spirit'. After punching in at half six, he sorted letters for three hours and was out on the street for the remaining five.

Pitching mail into slots did not necessitate immense concentration, so Bob usually accompanied the routine with a meditation, such as repeating the Jesus Prayer: 'Lord, Jesus Christ, have mercy on me a sinner.' He revealed that one of the best prayers he brought from the monastery came from the Good Friday liturgy: 'Father, I place my life in your hands.'

Those words released him to put his work at the mercy of God. Sometimes, when facing a problem in his own life, he would vary it with a prayer from the Easter Vigil: 'Christ, my Light, enlighten my darkness.' Or he would pray for someone in need, such as a hostage, or for a peaceful conclusion to a local or international crisis.

After sorting the mail, Bob would park his car at the start of the route. Then for ten minutes he would sit and read an entire text from his Bible. This kept him in a prayerful frame of mind and enabled him to dwell on a particular scriptural image or story as he set off with his trolley. He also memorised certain psalms and hymns, songs of the heart which kept him connected to the wider praying church as he went about his duties.

In some cases he found he had access to people and places clerical collars did not. For example, one day he learned of a tragedy which had engulfed a couple he knew from his rounds. The couple's sixteen-year-old son, who had struggled with cerebral palsy since birth, shot himself. Bob remembered driving over to the family and grieving with them but had felt helpless. For days afterwards, he found himself delivering many sympathy cards through their mail slot: 'I felt like I was standing on the outside of the Berlin Wall. There was all that pain and grief on the outside, and I felt so frustrated that I couldn't get to it.' He sent a couple of cards himself to the family, became a friend and, by sharing the painful situation with them, a 'very special and a very sacred' bond developed.

In one of his cards, Bob wrote that when he moved out of the monastery he had been faced with a dilemma: 'How in the world can I integrate being a "streetwalker" with my past orientation of a monk who has spent more time on his knees in a strict monastic enclosure? Ultimately, I resolved the seeming dichotomy by coming to this insight: In the monastery my focus was on seeking God. As a letter carrier, walking from house to house and from family to family, my vocation was no longer to seek the presence of God, but to *become* the presence of God. Far more demanding.'

Through original interviews, texts which have invigorated me and the struggles of my own unusual pilgrimage, this book explains how we might strive towards that. Bob said how moving from seeking God 'out there somewhere' to becoming the presence of God had been the 'breakthrough insight' that had literally revolutionised – from the Latin, *revolutus,* meaning 'to turn around' – his prayer life as he readjusted from the monastic milieu to the secular city. 'Ironically,' he added, 'this insight first came to me not in some ecstatic moment set aside for prayer, but while walking my mail route. I will see it always as the greatest gift given me by the people I served on my route. It was their stories and their openness to me that opened my eyes to what I was being called to be. Correction: become.'

It was clear to me that Bob had become what one might call 'a contemplative in the world', and his words inspired me to write the book. Spirituality grows out of a person's sense of identity, not from an ambition to be religiously superior to someone else. First and foremost Bob saw himself as a human being, but he received that humanity and identity by reflecting and praying.

Bob described his new role as a postman as one in which he could 'wear Christ'. He said he was a 'Christ-ed' *human being* missioned to make visible to others the presence of God. This was the very soul of ministry. He became part of people's stories and, through his ministry, learned the meaning and prayer of compassion. But it did not happen overnight.

Quick and easy solutions are not the usual way the spiritual life progresses. 'It is in the faithful, daily struggle that our identity in Christ is hammered out. But the final image that emerges is the more authentic and enduring for the persevering struggle.'

Bob realised that time and again. As he noted on one of his cards: 'Sorry the photos enclosed did not come out with good sharp image. But after all, that's a life's work, isn't it?'

1

Being Ourselves

The Benedictine writer, Mark Barrett, says that if the resurrection of the dead is anything like getting up in the morning he is not completely convinced that he wants to be included: he likes his sleep too much. 'Monks are neither the only early risers in our society, nor the earliest,' he points out. 'But, along with early morning radio presenters, it may be that we are among the most persistent.'[1]

I know what he means. When I worked as a newsreader at a large city radio station, I would always set my alarm for precisely 3.30 a.m. so I would arrive in time for the first shift. It was not really necessary to drag myself from my slumbers at what many might consider an unearthly hour, for the studios were only thirty minutes away. The reason I rose early was to pray alone in the chill of my study, in a corner of the room where a candle and an icon of the baptism of Christ had taken up permanent residence. A journalistic day that would be constructed around words had to emerge from complete silence.

As I clutched a mug of steaming tea and listened to intermittent solo rehearsals of the dawn chorus, I felt a connection with the early-rising nuns and monks around the world. Together we would offer the day to our Creator in the spirit of St Ambrose: 'Do you not know, my friend, that you owe the first fruits of your heart and voice to God? Run therefore to meet the rising sun so that when the day dawns it may find you ready.'[2]

It all seems a long time ago now and I do not think I have ever managed a more disciplined spiritual practice. The peace of heart that flowed from that silence sustained me through my formative life as a producer and presenter of broadcast news. It certainly gave my restless journalistic life a more stable monastic rhythm.

When I was on the late shift, before the last news bulletin of the day, I used take a prayerful stroll around the large empty TV studio close to the radio suite in Manchester. Although today it has been bulldozed into an uninspiring car park, it seemed then to possess all the wonder and mystery of a dark monastic church or a vast cathedral. Technicians might not have seen it that way, but I did and I didn't mind saying so.

I always sensed that the way I began and ended the journalistic day made all the difference to the manner in which I tried to live it, reporting on all the drama at the cutting edge of life and, perhaps like a priest, crossing the threshold of other people's lives at times of sorrow and joy. At a deeper level, however, perhaps I was responding to a personal vocation to live as a contemplative in the world. What encouraged me then was not the endorsement of a wise abbess or a shrewd hermit, but the friendship of many of my fellow journalists with whom I could share my monastic inclinations without embarrassment. On one occasion, during a training week in Leeds, I managed to get a group of editors together and persuaded them to meditate in unison. The sight of these tough, hard-talking news gurus closing their eyes and sitting in silence brought smiles to their faces at first but I think they came to engage with the spirit that motivated it.

I suppose that, in some ways, when I started out in journalism as a nineteen-year-old, it was like entering a novitiate. Intending it to be for life, I quietly claimed it as a calling since my work propelled me into hundreds of different human situations – to listen carefully, to bring truth to light and, when my stories made a organisation sit up and act, justice to the oppressed. When I moved into religious journalism, it was the churches' turn to be investigated and analysed.

There were many who might have questioned the work's divine origins but, some years later, after interviewing a Benedictine abbot and then being probed a little about my own life of faith, I was assured there was 'a distinct apostolate' within it and I should take it seriously. It was an unusual path in vocational terms but I learned to own my difference. As the contemplative and art historian Sister Wendy Beckett once put it: 'We must live the life we are actually given and use that specific life to come close to God.'[3]

In that classic text of the Orthodox Church, *The Way of the Pilgrim*, the author describes himself as 'a homeless wanderer of the humblest birth who roams from place to place'.[4] For me, as a writer, journalist and traveller, life has often seemed like that. Like the Pilgrim, whenever I head off, I usually take with me a black and tartan knapsack with the sewn-in words *No Fear*. I bought this in a shop near the Hotel Arts Barcelona, neither realising it was a hugely popular American lifestyle clothing brand, nor that, years later, a mother would stop me in the street and ask where she could buy one for her teenage son. So I feel quite cool as I trek about with the bag on my shoulder.

In other ways, though, the slogan has compelled me to have the courage to own my uniqueness and this is crucial if we are to be authentic pilgrims. We may need to resist strongly temptations or social pressures to conform, or play the game, if we are to be true to our deeper (contemplative) identity. Uniqueness has to be acknowledged and lived. The sixteenth-century Spanish poet and mystic St John of the Cross notes that God carries each person along a different road, so we are unlikely to find two people following the same route in even half of their journey to eternity.

This is Your Life

My little *No Fear* bag usually holds my MP3 player (with plenty of Bach and monastic chant), along with a small icon, crucifix and an ageing copy of *The Glenstal Book of Prayer*, a set of simple Benedictine offices which comes with me everywhere.[5] I have made this slim volume my own with a selection of prayer cards accumulated over the years. One of them is a laminated *Memorium* to the Irish broadcaster Eamonn Andrews who lived on the coast at Portmarnock, north of Dublin, until his death in 1987. Eamonn and I worked together on *This is Your Life* when I was twenty-one and he kept in touch with letters written in his distinctive emerald ink. It was my first job in broadcasting and, although I wasn't entirely prepared for the pragmatic world of television he seemed to inhabit so effortlessly, I looked up to Eamonn, not only as a towering figure of the small screen, but as a man of deep religious conviction.

On one occasion, during rehearsals for an edition of *This is Your Life*, to be recorded later in the day, I had to stand in for the unsuspecting subject, as researchers often did. Just before the familiar theme music struck up and we walked through the doors together, I heard Eamonn tell a member of the crew that he had come to the studios straight from Mass. It was not the kind of revelation usually heard backstage of a top TV show, but Eamonn wasn't nervous of declaring his allegiances in the sometimes irreverent world of light entertainment.

Eamonn had high standards outside the studios as well. If someone noticed him arriving for a church service near his home in the Chiswick area of London, they usually approached him to read one of the lessons, but invariably he would decline, explaining that he needed more time to prepare. Beside the statues and the candle stands, he saw himself not as a great star of television but as an ordinary pilgrim on a journey of faith. I still have a letter Eamonn sent me on the matter of vocation and the priesthood. In it, he reminded me gently that 'there are many ways of serving, and I feel sure you will find the best of them'.

I think about him sometimes when I am conducting a funeral in an independent capacity. The modern crematorium is reminiscent of a large studio and the service itself not unlike an edition of *This is Your Life* – each one is unique. The subject (the deceased) has had no input in the tribute being paid but family and friends are gathering to honour an individual. As I read from a prepared script, others sometimes join me at the lectern to add their 'live' recollections and occasionally there are messages from abroad. These are rarely stories from show business or sport, but from ordinary life that has made up the fabric of a community: the checkout assistant in Sainsbury's who had a smile for everyone, the polio sufferer with a gift for drawing Disney characters who raised over £10,000 for charity or the pantomime wardrobe mistress who proved to be the backbone of an entertainment society. Often we give thanks for longevity, but sometimes the circumstances are tragic, like the forty-year-old father who turned his life around and then died in a motorcycling accident.

While a funeral is a rite of passage where you commend that person to God, it is also an opportunity to bring them to life again for a while through a vivid tribute. In this respect, the experience of being a journalist has certainly been an advantage. Once, while visiting a bereaved family, my reporter's eyes fell upon the late mother's keys. They were lying on the table with an emblem bearing the words 'Do Deeds of Love'. I asked about this and learned that it had been the motto of the orphanage she had grown up in and around which she had built her life. So I constructed the service on the foundation of that one thought. I also discovered that her son was working in Saudi Arabia and that his Muslim friends had been praying for the family. So, as this gesture had an interfaith implication, I made a point of mentioning it early in the service and asked the congregation to pray for them.

I have come to realise that the *No Fear* on my rucksack actually complements those time-honoured words *This is Your Life*: we are called to live *our* life bestowed on us by God for the well-being of others through deeds of love. We are not expected to live somebody else's life or the life that somebody else – or some institution – thinks we should lead. The call of God is always personal. The Jesuit writer Karl Rahner believes people 'have a need to sing about themselves, about this ever new and unique person they are, each in their own way'.[6] The pastoral theologian Henri Nouwen writes about this in a series of imperatives to himself:

> Your unique presence in your community is the way God wants you to be present to others. Different people have different ways of being present. You have to know and claim your way ... God does not require of you what is beyond your ability, what leads you away from God, or what makes you depressed or sad. God wants you to live for others and to live that presence well. Doing so might include suffering, fatigue, and even moments of great physical or emotional pain, but none of this must ever pull you away from your deepest self and God.[7]

The Mystery of Silence

Being a contemplative, whether within the cloister, alone as a hermit or out in the world, involves aligning ourselves with a different understanding of time than we might be accustomed to. As someone schooled in the art of meeting deadlines, I was forced into some serious unlearning when I originally received the letters from my former Trappist correspondent. They began to unmask the hidden monk inside me; but at the same time, I felt my journalistic identity was indelible. Moreover, I was restless rather than static, never more alive than when I was vaulting around with my microphone or hammering out copy against the clock.

One evening, after returning home from another day of relentless news filing, I opened another package from the United States. Inside was a little hardback published as an accompaniment to *Chant*, a CD recorded by the Benedictine monks of Santo Domingo de Silos in northern Spain.

Authored by the Benedictine writer Brother David Steindl-Rast (with musician Sharon Lebell), *The Music of Silence* is a journey through the monastic seasons of the day: Vigils ('The Night Watch'), Lauds ('The Coming of the Light'), Prime ('Deliberate Beginning'), Terce ('Blessing'), Sext ('Fervour and Commitment'), None ('Shadows Grow Longer'), Vespers ('Lighting the Lamps'), Compline ('Completing the Circle') and The Great Silence ('The Matrix of Time').[8] The book shows how these hours are divine messengers, everyday angels that announce the gifts and challenges of each part of the day. Times of silence and deep listening give birth to inner peace in the heart. Chant is not so much an acoustic phenomenon as an inner experience, a reality more real than that experienced in our daily lives.

This eloquent book made me come alive in a completely new way. Dispatched by Bob at the peak of my days as a roving newshound, it taught me how to live in the present in a manner that was different from my journalistic reaction to the events of 'now'. At a time when my voice and name were on the radio regularly, reporting on current affairs, the book called me to a deeper response to life in the present as the 'eternal now'.

News is very much about the now. 'Breaking news' suggests that something significant is irrupting into our present. Journalists have their ears cocked and microphones primed to what is about to be announced. They're anxiously watching movements at a door or a window where a declaration is about to be made. But the 'eternal now', which chant heralds and beckons us to enter, could not be more contrasting. It invites us to stop, to listen, and to heed the message of *this* moment. 'It speaks to the monk in each of us, to our soul, which longs for peace and connection to an ultimate source of meaning and value,' writes Steindl-Rast, whose words underlined for me the dissimilarity between journalistic and monastic callings:

> Saturated with information but often bereft of meaning, we feel caught in a never-ending swirl of duties and demands, things to finish, things to put right. Yet as we dart anxiously from one activity to the next, we sense that there is more to life than our worldly agendas.
>
> Our uneasiness and our frantic scrambling are caused by our distorted sense of time, which seems to be continually running out. Western culture reinforces this misconception of time as a limited commodity. We are always meeting *dead*lines; we are always short on time, we are always running out of time.[9]

I blushed as I read what the monk had to say. I remembered an out-of-focus photograph of fairground swings which a film-maker friend had once given me and on which he had written: 'An image of your life?' Journalism is like one of those rides you just can't get off. The restless me was born for that life, but the contemplative me was also drawn by the music of silence. The serene yet soaring sounds of chant evoke a different relationship to time: the time available is in proportion to the task in hand, reminding us that there is another way to live *in* and *out of* time. 'Now' does not occur in chronological time but transcends it. Chant calls us to let go of our publicly constructed identity and reconnects us with our true self. As a journalist, I observed and I heard. As a contemplative, I would learn to see and to listen.

Contemplation does not solely concern concentrated periods of meditation but literally means 'a continuous putting together according to some measure'.[10] It connects the two realms of *chronos* (clock) time and *kairos* (eternal now) time. Those who lead a contemplative life are always measuring what they are doing in time against the now that does not pass away. They strive always to tune into the creative spirit of God and let it give shape to earthly reality. As Steindl-Rast notes:

> Contemplative life is the putting together of vision and action. Vision alone, meditation alone, is not true contemplation. We must put vision into action. Not just monks, but all of us are called to contemplation in this full sense. If we want to live healthy lives, we have to build into our daily life moments of vision, and then let our action be formed by that vision. Listening to chant can be a moment in which we open our inner eyes to the vision that needs to be enacted.[11]

In ordinary life, we are tempted to measure things subjectively in terms of earthly success, achieving our goals or fulfilling someone else's expectations. But our lives have depth and meaning only when we view them from a higher vantage point: the eternal now. It is a journey that abandons reaction in favour of response to what is before us in each moment.

Steindl-Rast believes that one of the reasons we feel so unsettled in our daily lives is because we are either ruminating on the past or agonising about the future. We are, therefore, never present in the here and now where our real selves reside. Chant calls us out of chronological time, in which 'now' can never be located, and into the eternal now, which is not really found *in* time. Eternity is not a long, long time. It is no time. We cannot reach that 'now' by proceeding in a chronological sequence, yet it is accessible at any moment as the mysterious fullness of time. We are welcomed into time's mystery in our peak experiences when we say such things as 'time seemed to stand still' or 'we spoke for hours but it just seemed like a flash'. Writing can be like that as well. Brother David comments:

> Our sense of time is altered in those moments of deep and intense experience, and so we know what now means. We

feel at home in that now, in that eternity, because that it is the only place where we really *are*. We cannot *be* in the future and we cannot *be* in the past; we can only *be* in the present. We are only real to the extent to which we are living in the present here and now.[12]

The Music of Silence became a faithful companion, like a loyal Labrador leading me into unexplored territories of the soul and joining me on my foreign assignments. More significantly, I think it encouraged me to think about stepping back from reporting life as it was being lived in order to capture a deeper reality. Something similar happened to Jack Good. Jack was the television producer who introduced rock 'n' roll to Britain. But, at the height of his fame, he faced an existential crisis and announced he was quitting show business to become a hermit-iconographer in the wilds of America. 'I believe that the purpose of life is to glorify God and this is going to be my way of trying to do it,' he announced.

At the same time as he had been discovering such pop idols as Cliff Richard, Tommy Steele and Billy Fury in the 1960s, Jack had been deepening his journey of faith by entering the Roman Catholic Church. Eamonn Andrews, who was his sponsor, became godfather to three of his children. But after Eamonn later surprised him as the guest of honour for *This is Your Life*, Jack began to have doubts about his showbiz leanings and realised his life could be spiritually richer. So he headed off to New Mexico as a painter in order to get in touch with his deeper self. But wildernesses are not utopias and solitude does not always produce serenity. In the new desert landscape, Jack wrestled with guilt over the music culture he had midwifed but now loathed. One of his paintings depicted television in the form of the devil. He was also forced to confront many other demons, which included his drinking and the break-up of his marriage. Jack later returned to England and now, in his eighties, continues his eremitical life in an Oxfordshire barn. With his bushy grey beard and habit, he prays for people in need and for the mercy of God on his extraordinary life.

Jack Good is not the only showbiz legend to have been drawn to the world of contemplation. In her later life, the Oscar-winning actress Patricia Neal was healed of her wounds through the ministrations of a Benedictine community in Connecticut. There the prioress, Mother Dolores Hart, was herself a former film actress who had starred with Elvis Presley. Another Hollywood star, June Haver, spent several months testing her vocation in a convent, while Jane Wyman was buried in a habit because she had been a member of the Third Order of the Dominicans.

The Attraction of Opposites

In between shooting movies, Anthony Minghella was another cinematic figure who sought solace and another form of direction at a Benedictine community on the Isle of Wight, close to where he had grown up. After interviewing him at London's Abbey Road studios, where he was perfecting the soundtrack to *Cold Mountain*,[13] he urged me to visit Quarr Abbey. Eventually the day came when I was boarding a ferry at Portsmouth. As *St Faith* set off boldly into the dark, rain-lashed waters, I stood on deck and knew I had to make the journey. As the ferry neared its destination, I could see the bell tower in the distance. But any flutters of excitement were tamed by anxiety. Attraction and fear were locked in an awkward embrace. In monasteries, you find out things about yourself you would rather not face.

Had it not been for Minghella, I might have gone to the movies instead that weekend. But he persuaded me it was his favourite spiritual place and that I should try it out. 'It has simplicity, it is overpoweringly beautiful and is so fuss-free,' he had enthused. 'You walk into its atmosphere and it's tangible, palpable, and really it's such a haven I can't possibly recommend it enough.' Although no stranger to the Benedictine way of life, nearly two years had passed before I managed to take up his suggestion. By the time I got round to carrying my bulky bag up the cone-laden bridle path at Fishbourne towards the cloisters, he was hard at work on another film with Jude Law, *Breaking and Entering*,[14] about an architect who encounters a thief and starts to re-evaluate his life. I was about to re-evaluate mine.

As I turned left down a path to the courtyard, I cast my mind back to what Minghella had said about the place. 'They take great pride in their food but they carry their eating implements with them. There's this wonderful moment where they delve inside their habits and out come forks, knives and spoons. They eat and clean their bowls with these rather large napkins, then everything disappears again. It's like a magician's act but it's to assert simplicity, order and routine.' I was soon to witness the performance.

Ever since I was a teenage reporter, I had been drawn to monastic communities but had never fully understood why, although I sensed it had something to do with an attraction of opposites. I had never found the transition easy and pangs of loneliness invariably enveloped me as I opened the door of the guest room. Whenever I saw a white sink, a slither of green soap, a religious painting or two on the wall and a crucifix above the bed, I wanted to be gone. I think it had something to do with the fear of being alone with the Alone.

My short retreats have always been double-edged. And yet, as soon as I leave, I want to be back there again. For me, they can be transformative experiences because you are never quite the same person after you've been on a monastic retreat. In monasteries, you are forced to confront your own paradoxes. For Anthony Minghella, it was about an attraction to regimes because he said he did not have one. 'I feel drawn to rules and I feel drawn to routine because my life is so empty of rules and routine,' he confessed. 'It's partly to do with my inability to sustain order and because essentially I feel I am trying to contain the chaos that I create. I am trying to put some shape to it. I don't think I'm very different from anybody else really. We are all struggling with the mess we make for ourselves.'

I knew what he meant. Like film-making, journalism, too, is about shaping order out of chaos, constructing reports out of conflicting facts, obstructions and diverse opinions, jigsawing profiles from the fragments of a disparate life. As with any occupation, the pressures of broadcasting or film production can swiftly divert you from your own inner life. Visiting a monastery, therefore, leads to an engagement with a deeper reality which is hard to ignore or evade. Minghella found it frightening because most of us fell so far short of that kind of life. It could be intimidating, several times a day, to be with people who had devoted their entire life to the belief that the inner being was more important than the outer one. They paid little attention to external issues but had an overwhelming sense of belief in function.

When Minghella was on retreat at Quarr, he looked forward to the periods of silence when he could take stock. He said there was so little time 'in the lives we have created for ourselves, and in the world we have created for ourselves' for any form of meditation to be built into a day. But 'these men – who are surprisingly worldly, surprisingly in touch with what is going on outside of the monastery, and surprisingly human – have this clarity in their expression and in their thinking which comes from building into a life this interesting flexing between a requirement that they work in quite functional tasks and a requirement that each day is punctuated by periods of reflection and prayer.'

The writer and director, who bore more than a passing resemblance to Thomas Merton, told me that one of the requirements of visiting his parents in Ryde was that, the morning after he arrived home, they all had to walk up to the abbey, sit and think, then go back for breakfast or lunch. It had become part of his journey to the island. He found a need to speak to some of the monks and refresh himself. The practice of breaking off from his work and entering into silence had fascinated him through-out his life. The attraction of a retreat was the spiritual equivalent of a health farm. But like a physical fitness programme, it might be hard to sustain, so it was daunting to realise there was an abbot and his monks who lived that way all the time.

'It probably gives people like me a glimpse of what one could be like but isn't, so it's an enormously refreshing change from the chaos and madness which goes on outside of the abbey,' he remarked. 'That's what you notice immediately: you're in a place that has existed for almost a thousand years, the same lifestyle has been going on there, and the imprimatur of that is very, very tangible. You feel there is a rhythm, routine and contemplation that has gone on for so long and will go on after you.

'There are these wonderful trees around the abbey and they've been there for a long time too. There's a sense of establishment and comfort, but not privilege. There's something so functional and that has always appealed to me. It's the equivalent of the music that I always associate when I say the word "Quarr". I hear something. I hear this Gregorian chant which permeates the experience of being there, this wonderful sound that comes out. The church is enormously resonant because it has so little interference or obstruction within its space and, just like the chant, which could not be more simple but which contains this lava of emotion, belief and spirituality, so the building and the sense of the place does that for me too.

'All of the clichés about monastic life are true – there's an enormous serenity and mischief simultaneously. It's not surpris-ing that so many writers of fiction have created mischievous, cherubic monks because I think there's tension between a sense of play, that seems to me present in them, together with a very,

very profound spirituality. If you look at all spiritual practices, it's interesting that in the oriental religions, Buddhas laugh, and I think really profound spiritual people experience a dialectic between the degree of spiritual centre they have and their ability to laugh. I see that in all of these monks.'

But of all the many entertaining descriptions Anthony Minghella painted of Quarr, there was one I held on to. It made me reflect on what it meant to become the presence of God for others. What he said was phrased in the form of a contradiction: the degree of contemplation in a monastery reflects the degree of empathy. 'It's not solipsism,' he explained. 'Sometimes in the secular world, meditation confuses itself with the idea that you are the centre of something, that somehow it takes you into yourself. But the contemplation practised by Benedictines takes you out into a profound empathy with other people's suffering and with what's going on in the world. It's not at all about contemplating your navel. It's about contemplating the suffering and the spirit of others. It's very much about giving your self enough time to devote your self to others.'

One of the first books I noticed in the guest house library was Thomas Merton's *No Man is an Island,* in which the Trappist monk makes a similar point. The Isle of Wight seemed an appropriate place to muse on what he writes – an island away from the mainland but part of the whole. Merton says that our life (as individuals and as members of the struggling, human race) provides us with the evidence that it must have meaning. Our purpose is to discover the meaning and live according to it. We have, therefore, something to live *for*. The process of living, of growing up and becoming a person is the gradually increasing awareness of what that 'something' is. But the truth never becomes clear so long as we assume that each one of us, individually, is the centre of the universe. We do not exist for ourselves alone and it is only when we are fully convinced of this fact that we begin to love ourselves properly and to love others too. If we live for others, Merton argues, we will come to discover that no one expects us to be 'as gods'. We will see that we are human like everyone else, that all of us have different weaknesses and deficiencies, and that such limitations actually play a crucial part in our lives. It is precisely because of them that we need others and others need us. So our successes are not our own because the way to them is prepared by others and the fruit of our labours is not our own because we are preparing the way for the achievement of others. Nor are our failures our own because they may spring from the failure of another. But they are also compensated for by another's achievement. Therefore, says Merton:

> Every other man is a piece of myself, for I am part and a member of mankind. Every Christian is part of my own body, because we are members of Christ. What I do is also done for them and with them and by them. What they do is done in me and by me and for me. But each of us remains responsible for his own shore in the life of the whole body. Solitude, humility, self-denial, action and contemplation, the sacraments, the monastic life, the family, war and peace – none of these make sense except in relation to the central reality which is God's love living and acting in those whom He has incorporated in His Christ. Nothing at all makes sense, unless we admit, with John Donne, that: 'No man is an island, entire of itself; every man is a piece of the continent, a part of the main.'[15]

In terms of interior growth, a stay in a monastery doesn't tend to produce immediate changes or an obvious sense that the course of your life has been put back on track. Nothing may appear to happen. But this is not the point. We consent to be changed by that 'central reality' and, like a seed in the earth, the movement is slow and imperceptible. While I was at Quarr, it was Pentecost, the season when the church celebrates the coming of the Holy Spirit. It has always been a special time of year for me because I was born on Whit Monday, the day after

Pentecost. After a splendid lunch with the brothers, but drinking only water, I attended the afternoon office of None and then made my way back to Fishbourne, clambering aboard a ferry bound for the mainland. It was a calmer crossing that day and, as I looked back at the island receding behind me, I felt euphoric in an inebriated kind of way. I thought at first it must have been the wine I had consumed over the meal at lunchtime – but then I remembered that I had remained sober because I would be driving later. Yet the feelings continued. I concluded that, on Pentecost Sunday, I was experiencing what is known as 'spiritual drunkenness', when you are so filled with the Holy Spirit that you become light-headed and even sometimes fall over.

The time itself at Quarr had seemed rather dry but the fruit was to come later. I was sorry to leave though and had felt a little bereft, for the brothers and I had bonded in silence through the Spirit. The intoxication was proof of that and it was sufficiently overwhelming to share later with my spiritual director.

A monastery is a place where God keeps an eye on you. It is where you refuel spiritually. And the journalist in me has discovered that many a good story lurks behind a cowl or veil.

2

The Madness of Love

When he was a hermit in a house on stilts on a Pacific island, Matthew Kelty learned the need to listen to the God 'hidden in the quiet of your own abandoned heart'.[1] But he recognised that that could be difficult, even in such an exotic wilderness, because what emerged from the heart was not always good company. 'Come into the shambles of my heart, dear Lord; come into the shanty I call home,' he would pray at the time of Holy Communion as he asked God for mercy and grace to heal him.[2] If it were not possible for him to tidy up his heart on his own, it was vital that he got to know it, so he could live in the truth.

Kelty had few clothes while he was living in Papua New Guinea. He learned to wash them by hauling water and scrubbing on a board. Fenced in by pineapple plants and banana groves, he stuck to a diet of rice, cheese, fish and soda crackers (he called them 'sea biscuits') and drew spiritual energy from the wonders of the natural world: suns rising and setting, the sea, wind, stars and woods. There was little else to divert him – after all, that was the point of being apart from everyone else. Kelty felt that so much noise in contemporary society drowned out the inner capacity for dialogue with God. On the island, he came to learn that people are by nature contemplatives.

Papua New Guinea was one of two remaining United Nations' trust territories, administered by Australia. A year after the monk's arrival, it achieved independence and self-government. With a population of 2.6 million, there were around a thousand different tribes divided into hundreds of language groups.

Letters from a Hermit tells the story of his journey into solitude with a flute and a set of books by Carl Jung among his few possessions.[3] Although he was the only monk on New Guinea, his correspondence from the time reveals he was totally at home with the islanders – real people, 'in touch with their heart' and 'such a contrast to head-centred Westerners. ... The whole primitive style was one foot on earth, one foot in the world of the spirit – in everything. What Western man offers them is pretty one-footed on earth and that's it. Even in religion there is little opening for the mystic dimension, very little.'[4]

Kelty discovered that the people themselves were 'of a mind with the monks' and he had come to say to them 'I am with you'. They were spiritual people and everyday life was permeated with religion. 'They know they have a soul and they live as if the soul mattered.'[5] Moreover, he was not cautious in declaring that Papua New Guinea and its 'primitive life' had actually opened him up to the contemplative life which was natural on the island. He was where he belonged and he hoped he could swing it. Nights were superb, dawns elegant, dusks rich. But under the 'noonday demon', everything seemed flat and spiritless, killed and drenched in white heat and light.

Over the course of nearly a decade, Kelty was exposed to human poverty and the need of mercy. It opened him to the mystery of the universal, human heart. It was difficult at times getting to know himself but he could only feel gratitude:

> I think the role of obedience is to help us to remain loyal to the truth and to help us to discover God's truth, another way of saying, our own. That problem, in our terms, is always the false self, the make-believe self, the self we have constructed. This is a relatively harmless business in a life of no great depth or intensity, but once you move into something a little serious, it can become a snag ... Certainly in your own life obedience is just as vital in that you must, if you are to attain to your freedom, your destiny, respond wholly to God's will, which

is to say, be truly yourself. The problem lies in trying to discern that true self, to find freedom road and walk it. Here we are much deceived often enough, assuming that we know who we are and what we are to do. Thus, there is to be some sort of deference to God's will that is almost total: I say almost total to indicate that it is not mere 'submission' but something we work out, we do, we unravel day by day. Purity of heart, as the old monks used to say, is the secret: being clean. Not devious or scheming. Honest in everything. I am quite sure that God's will can be discerned, and correctly, but one must be totally open to whatever it be, available.[6]

Kelty spent hours alone on the shore or in his house praying and reading. The need for time and space was a birthright that should always be protected. He believed we all benefitted from hours of peace to ponder and dwell, to let things be. Solitude was an opportunity to put the tools down, seal your lips, turn the lights out and the music off, and listen – to the wind, your breathing, the divine presence in the soul. For him, life was a total gift.

A novice under Merton and later his confessor, Matthew Kelty has been inspirational in encouraging me to try to live more contemplatively. He was, in fact, the first person to greet me when I turned up at Our Lady of Gethsemani monastery, hidden in the tree-covered hills of Kentucky, to learn more about Merton for a radio programme. He was clearly an impressive individual in his own right, a renowned spiritual teacher, priest and counsellor who, at ninety-three, was still seeking to grow deeper every day in his relationship with Christ, an ongoing love affair without parallel this side of eternity. In his eyes, the purpose of monastic life was to discover reality which removed from your vision anything that was false and fraudulent, artificial and constructed. That was most people's goal, he maintained, so monks should not be regarded as freaks for trying.

In his chapter talks, Kelty sometimes alluded to the beguiling power of chant. He compared the rituals of the Divine Offices and the procession of the monks with the native ceremonial dances that had held him spellbound in the South Pacific. Dancing, he believed, got people into the rhythm of the universe. The natives caught that rhythm – unlike Christians. 'Choir is primarily song and dance,' he told his brethren:

> Song it surely is. It is a formalized dance, a stylized one, quiet and contemplative in character rather than ecstatic. It does not involve a great deal of movement, but there is rhythm nonetheless in a large number of group actions and postures. There is [Latin] the language from another time, from our ancestors. There is also the music from our forebears, having a peculiarly religious character because of its use for centuries in worship. The whole adds up to a creation of staggering beauty: the cowls, the psalters, the strange melody and awesome chanting back and forth between the two facing choirs, the bowing and rising and sitting and standing. All this makes an impression that is never forgotten.[7]

When the monks seek God, they find him, said Kelty. And when they find him, they need not worry about them singing and dancing. By entering into the rhythm, they touch the heart of life. We all dance to the rhythm of our heartbeat, to our every breath, our every step.

> We dance to each passing hour whether in a field of corn, doing the wash, cooking the soup or sewing socks. We all dance. The thing is to dance well and make explicit the monastic song and dance of the love that is in us. The choir as we know it may not be essential to monastic life but love is. The choir is simply an expression of that love, an expression that is ancient and beauteous, most thoroughly in keeping with the deepest religious instincts of humankind.[8]

Monks at Gethsemani have been singing for the coming of the kingdom since December 1848. The chanting goes on seven times a day, seven days a week. In the midst of a violent and hostile universe, the brothers intone those ancient songs for their own healing and the healing of the world. Although Kelty was convinced that, fundamentally, monastic living was a serious business, he could not deny its madness. He said he lived in a mad house, full of mad men. What could be madder than going off into the wilderness, putting up a wall, staying behind it and keeping the world out? What was more bizarre than getting up at two in the morning, putting on great cowls and cloaks and spending hours every day singing songs to God in a forgotten tongue and melody? What could be more strange than being celibate and virginal, never marrying, drinking beer or watching TV, yet subject to an authority whose whim or wish, order or command, is law, binding not only in the practical order but also in the realm of soul? 'The people who do these things must be out of their minds. Or else they are in love,' he said. 'They do mad things because people who are in love do mad things. There is no other way that love can speak. This is the language of love. It is not necessary. It is not reasonable. It is not in accord with common sense. All very true. It is simply the way of people who are in love.'⁹

Kelty struck me as an utterly natural human being, without pretence or artifice. There was nothing remotely clerical about him. His life was a love affair with God. In one of his addresses, he told retreatants: 'We're in this together, honey. It's a communal endeavour. You're not going to heaven alone.'¹⁰ This surely is the secret of Christian living. We have to travel together, helping one another to carry the luggage.

Some likened Kelty's style to that of a Celtic monk of early Christianity. He chuckled at the allusion; he had Irish roots himself. His family came to America in the 1840s after the Great Famine and settled in 'the Irish hills' of Detroit. Born in 1915, Kelty grew up in Milton, Massachusetts. He developed a love of poetry at school, but classes in medieval history stimulated an early monastic inclination. He later joined an enterprising and dynamic missionary order, the Divine Word Society. Ordained a priest in 1946, he was sent to New Guinea where he made trips into the bush, gave instruction, offered Mass and dispensed medicine. It was a hard, lonely existence for a natural introvert. Returning to the United States to edit the order's magazine, he felt drawn to the cloistered life. When publication was suspended because of an office fire, he was able to make a retreat at Gethsemani and later entered the community in February 1960. His novice training under Merton was rigorous – this was still in the days when the monks slept on straw mattresses (an historic hangover rather than an explicitly monastic practice). Kelty recalled that the monastery smelt of incense and wet wool because they didn't open the windows during the winter and had very little heat.

Gethsemani was a place geared to the flourishing of the inner life, a world of communion with God and prayer, and worship through the beauty of chant, sung in the offices of the day – and all of it sustained by a community of sixty or so that enabled the *opus Dei* (the work of God) to be carried out. It might not have been the group he would have chosen as friends, but they were there as brothers to love. Like him, they were flawed. You practise love, he would say, and after a decade or two you get fairly good at it. When you enter the order, you don't know the landscape of your own heart. Like marriage, it is an adventure of faith and love is the only quality that makes it workable.

Kelty saw beyond the theatricality of monastic life. A monk was not just his daily performance. There was behind every cowl something real and immortal, touched with and possessed by the divine, wrapped in God's presence. But he also acknowledged that a monk was someone shrouded in darkness; within him strange forces were at war. A monk was a person tossed by moods and emotions, tainted with despair and envy, tempted by pride and power. Such forces could lie dormant until aroused.

34

Only after years of righteous living within the scrupulous eye of a loving community could a monk's passions be brought into control and his moral life into order. Then a new aspect of the monk emerged, the other side of his being. Having learned how poor he really was, he could rejoice in the love of God and his redemption through Christ:

> The experience of God's love becomes very real indeed and a great sense of compassion for others begins to grow into significant dimensions. An experience of compassion comes from having drunk deeply of human misery in your own heart. It is no great trick to accept others once you have accepted yourself. But to accept others without having done the same act of mercy to your own self is simply impossible. 'Love your neighbour as yourself,' he said.[11]

Over the years, Kelty had taken on a range of roles, from monastery cobbler to director of vocations. But feeling drawn to a deeper solitude, the possibilities of a hermit life appealed to him. After experimenting with different forms of community life away from the monastery, he eventually received permission to live in Papua New Guinea as a solitary. He left New York by ship on 19 November 1973 and arrived on Christmas Eve. For a while he lived in a mission station but eventually had his hermitage built. After almost ten years, Kelty returned permanently to the community in Kentucky, bringing with him the experience of solitude and all that it had taught him. More than anything else, what this monk taught me is that all that ultimately matters is to be known and loved by God.

Matthew Kelty prayed to God that, before he died, he would make at least one act of pure love for Him. He said he kept practising but believed there was no finer thing to do this side of eternity. Shortly after noon on Friday, 18 February 2011, he died peacefully in the monastery's infirmary following a spell in hospital. After Thomas Merton, he is arguably the monastery's most famous inhabitant, with his sermons published in several volumes and DVDs of his life and times on sale in the monastery shop. Yet as he reflected: 'We all want to be significant but the contemplative life says that, well, we are significant, but that is not really what counts – being famous, well-known or even remembered. To spend a lifetime learning the art of love and particularly the art of the love of God is a worthy life.' That was what holiness and sanctity meant to him.

Hermitage Within

Like many monks, Kelty was a divine searcher rather than a self-seeker. When a friend asked to write a biography of him, he replied: 'If you do it or not, it makes no difference.'[12]

In a similar spirit of self-effacement, when a hermit, believed to be Swiss, was having talks with a publisher about a book on his hidden life in the mountains, he refused to divulge his name. So when *The Hermitage Within* reached the bookshops, potential readers gleaned only that it had been written by 'A Monk'.[13] In a note along with his manuscript, the modest monastic warned the editor: 'Not everyone, obviously, can and should live as a monk or hermit. But no Christian can do without an inner hermitage in which to meet his God.'[14]

The book was a compelling read at a time when I was re-engaging with a contemplative way of living. But I needed a sacred space where I could spend time alone with God. It wasn't practical to build a shack in the middle of a forest, while a corner of a room set aside for prayer was not sufficient. I needed somewhere I could visit but was close enough for the support of family and friends after a bewildering episode in my life. My brother had recently moved into a large cottage with a sprawling garden a mile or so from the family home. He wasn't using one of the old workshops and offered it to me as a sanctuary. Not only that, he painted the walls and spruced things up with a fresh carpet and new chair. I didn't want it to be too comfortable, but over the course of several weeks the vices and benches were taken out and the icons and candles installed. A spare CD player boomed out chant, a golden bowl wafted out incense and I sat in the chair studying *The Hermitage Within*.

Even though I was only reading and entering metaphorically, the opening words were scary for a writer: 'To influence others directly, even by the pen, is not one of the pursuits envisaged for the desert,' warned the anonymous monk, as though he had been tipped off about what his reader did. 'You must be content to lose yourself entirely. If you secretly desire to be or to become "somebody", you are doomed to failure.'[15]

In spite of what you have read and 'what you call your experience', you will not know what the loneliness of the desert has in store for you, I was informed.

There, as elsewhere, no two souls follow precisely the same path, and God never repeats himself in his creatures. Very rarely, if at all, does he reveal his designs in advance. 'Humble and detached, go into the desert. For God, awaiting you there, you bring nothing worth having, except your entire availability. The lighter your human baggage is, the poorer you will be in what the world esteems, and the greater will be your chances of success, since God will be all the freer to use you. He is calling you to live on friendly terms with him: to nothing else.[16]

As I read tentatively through the pages, I came to recognise that any kind of contemplative attitude has to be prefaced by a total giving of one's self to God. This is something that can only happen in silence and will unfold in its own time. Nothing can be forced, predicted or assumed. The early days or weeks in your cell will reveal very little, perhaps nothing. Humbly accept the boredom, says the hermit, the pacing to and fro. The heart is still raw from everything that has been left behind and there is still tumult in the imagination and emotions to be 'enthralled by the Invisible'.[17] The austerity and ennui might tempt you to run away, the wise man senses, but you will find nothing outside. All the riches of the desert, mountain and temple which define the solitary would be instantly lost if he walked away. The cell is a shelter from the flux of the world, a *poustinia* or inner desert where God pays secret visits to the soul and where the soul waits in a spirit of recollection for him. Here, released from the burdens of the world, the hermit 'begins his eternity rejoicing in the Lord'.[18] If you are generous with your heart, you might begin to see the divine world emerging from the shadows, he concludes, and you will discover that you are never less alone than when you are alone.

Whether or not you follow such experienced guidance in a building devoted to prayer, or within the one you are carving out in your own heart, it is clear that the interior journey is one which, carefully and openly undertaken, will eventually lead to an intimacy with the divine through silence and a greater awareness of the interconnectedness of all things. During my first weeks in the newly created hermitage, I noticed the colour and patterns of butterflies more than ever before. One of them emerged from behind the night storage heater and took up residence around the borders of an icon of the Virgin and Child. It stayed there for days and, even after flying out through the door, flitted around for weeks and seemed to follow me everywhere, especially when I went for prayer walks around the pear and apple orchard. The hours spent in silent encounter and recollection, while both demanding and inconsequential at the time, made me more focused and alive as I interacted with nature more purposefully. When leading a retreat, for example, I noticed a wounded butterfly in the room. It darted about during discussions but on the last morning, when I was alone, the creature died in front of me – though not before I had blessed it for the onward journey. Becoming the presence of God for others is not just about people.

I found myself engaging in sharper conversations with people who came in and out of my life. It was undoubtedly a time of trial on occasions, but only afterwards did I become aware that some interior progress had been made. I continued to take funerals for friends. I seemed more attentive during the half-hour slot at the crematorium than I had ever been before. I was aware of a greater calmness within me which I believe communicated itself to mourners, especially during difficult services when the deceased person had died in particularly distressing circumstances. I had always known that I was more a contemplative than a cleric; these titles are not, of course, mutually exclusive. I think my time spent being guided by women in religious orders over many years has given birth to my deeper sense of calling.

The eucharist, in whatever tradition it is celebrated, has always lain at the heart of my spiritual life. When I was growing up, an older friend used to say: 'I don't go to church. I go from it.' He meant that, after receiving the Body of Christ in the form of bread and wine, he went out into the world as a walking sacrament. A Benedictine monk explains that the eucharist is the privileged place where the church is able to recognise 'the Prince of life' (Acts 3:15) who was offered up as a victim for the sins of the world. He goes on: 'The living signs of his resurrection are when we meet together under his leadership, recall his words and the words of scripture, recount the testimony of those who saw him, joyfully break bread and then head off again into the world where the tiny flame, which was enkindled at the first Eastertide, is spread from person to person.'[19] This might also be understood of becoming the presence of God to others.

It has surprised me how many people find silence unsettling, perhaps because it obliges them to undertake an inner journey they would rather not make. Some people in the church seem to think that silence is something you do on your own because collectively it is embarrassing. This is because there is no learning and teaching about the way God communicates to us in silence. Maggie Ross comments:

> The tragedy of contemporary institutional religion, pre-occupied as it is with the power struggles of the clergy, is that it has become part of the kingdom of noise. It has forgotten its task of bringing the transfiguring silence of adoration into the static world of discord. If adoration is not the foundation of the institution's service, then that service all too frequently becomes predatory and degrading to those it hopes to serve.[20]

Many of us will be familiar with the talking that goes on in churches before a service begins. Even though others have their heads unmistakeably bowed in silence, the chatter persists, sometimes gathering so much momentum that it is impossible to continue being focused in prayer. You don't have that irruption in a hermitage or monastery. You sometimes hear it said that people just aren't comfortable with silence, but this can be a projection of the person claiming it. I remember praying with a deeply committed ninety-year-old and ending with a time of quiet. I then sat back in my chair in case it was long enough for her but she wasn't perturbed and carried on praying. Afterwards her first comment was 'I liked that silence'.

To become the presence of God in the world, we have to home ourselves in that interior cloister. We are then filled with a silence that will continue to run through our spiritual veins as we comfort someone going through a depression, visit a neighbour with ovarian cancer or stand up for justice on an ethical matter in a Christian context. Whatever form our ministry takes, it will be infused with the contemplative if it emerges from that silence. Brother Wayne Teasdale, who lived as an urban monk in the world, integrating Western and Eastern spiritual traditions, says:

> The important work for all of us in the world is the inner struggle and refinement that goes on in the midst of our daily

activities. How do we succeed in dwelling in the cave of our own hearts, in that monastery within? How do we nurture and nourish, inspire and inform, the inner monk that all of us have, and *are*, as an expression of the mystic in us?[21]

This interior engagement is replenished through the regular spiritual practices we can manage sensibly and these form part of our everyday routine. There are many different ways of praying but none of these should be forced. The well-quoted maxim of the Benedictine abbot Dom John Chapman – 'Pray as you can, not as you can't' – rings true. I have a friend who feels she can only really pray when out walking her dog – her mind is distracted if she sits at home.

The set offices of the church can provide an undercurrent to people's spiritual lives and many are nourished by saying them. But at times there are just too many words. Now that I have returned to a more silent practice, I find that reflecting on just a few lines of scripture from the set readings, in front of an icon and candle, carries me through the day. I keep returning to these words and allow them to penetrate my being, whether sitting in front of a microphone, stacking the dishwasher or reclining at the dentist's. For example, this morning I chose from the weekday missal a verse from Jeremiah about those who trust in the Lord being 'like a tree by the waterside that thrusts its roots to the stream: when the heat comes it feels no alarm, its foliage stays green; it has no worries in a year of drought, and never ceases to bear fruit' (Jeremiah 17:8, *Jerusalem Bible*). What more do I need? These words will stay with me until my head hits the pillow tonight. Even if I am not consciously aware of them during the day, I know that something will be happening inside.

It matters not a jot how we pray but only that we remain connected with God, uneventful though the experience may seem to be. All our lowly God yearns for is faithfulness to our loving relationship with Him. Once we begin evading our prayer discipline because we haven't time or find it boring, then our day will not be the same. I always remember an Orthodox priest, who had been a monk on Mount Athos for twenty-two years, telling me how God was more humble than we could possibly imagine. He was there waiting at the appointed hour set by us: 'My spiritual father used to say to me: "If you have a rule to pray before three and four o'clock in the morning, God is there like a lover waiting for you. But if you sleep during that period, wake up at half past four and expect God to be there, like a lover he's gone."'

3

Hollowed Out

One spring morning, after we had been praying together at her home, a friend placed into my hand a chain with a medal of St Christopher, the patron saint of travellers. She had found it among her jewellery and asked if I would like it as a form of protection because I am always on the move. It speaks to me of my inner journey as well. It also reminds me of the day I was heading across New York in a yellow cab when the driver showed me his electronic version of the medal. As he broke the speed limit, a figure on his dashboard lit up and an American voice thundered: 'This is St Christopher. You're on your own now.'

In a more profound sense, the chain is helping me to become who I am. A Trappistine nun, who has illumined my understanding of the contemplative life, believes that 'becoming' is the essence of any spiritual journey. The traveller is 'the substance' of this adventure into God, a movement characterised by a dynamic transformation of being as we immerse ourselves in the mystery.

A former abbess of a Cistercian monastery in a remote part of Canada, where she still resides, Sister Jean-Marie Howe says the key to any journey's authenticity is *depth*, in which 'doing' is always at the service of 'becoming'. We move towards depth, within depth and out of depth.[1]

Human existence is a journey that begins and ends in God, even though 'in God' there can be no terminus as we go on growing. We have our part to play in its unfolding for we are at liberty to become who we are or not. While it is unnecessary to

43

travel far and wide on the interior search, what remains essential is to *return within*, for this is the true terrain of the spiritual journey. Christ calls us to come and see where he dwells, not 'up there', but within our own hearts.

Howe tells us that the human soul is inhabited with a longing, a yearning for its homeland and that life here on earth, as beautiful as it may be, is, in some sense, both an exile and a pilgrimage. If it is true that 'home is where the heart is', and that our hearts are indeed restless until they rest in God, could it be, she suggests, that 'home' is not a *place*, be it terrestrial or celestial, but rather a *relationship*, a loving relationship of the human person with God?

Could it be that within the depths of this relationship we find our way home because we have found God, or better yet, because we have let God find us? Perhaps this is a lesson we all have to learn in time, especially if we have been wounded by or feel alienated from the church in some way. The place doesn't ultimately matter – but the relationship does.

Great artists can teach us so much about the movement of the spiritual life, not only by their works but also through their words. When friends were urging the French sculptor Auguste Rodin to finish a project, he forestalled them by his insistence on not hurrying. A solitary figure, always in harmony with the elemental power and steady rhythm of the natural world, Rodin sensed his sculptures could only come to birth through the disciplines of silence and patience. 'He possessed the quiet perseverance of men who are necessary, the strength of those for whom a great work is waiting,' noted his secretary, the poet Rainer Maria Rilke.[2]

Contemplative living requires a similar fortitude. Nothing can be forced or rushed. We have to learn the art of waiting and allow ourselves to become a vacuum. We are so conditioned to expectation or results that prayer can appear meaningless. But whenever I feel frustrated or even bored, I remember the nun who said to me: 'I have been here since 1955 and I am still waiting for something to happen.' Our relationship with God, formed in secret, does not always have visible signs of growth.

The English sculptor Henry Moore is known for his semi-abstractions of reclining human figures and their hollow spaces. One of them, *Mother and Child: Hollow*, is a powerful visual symbol of our journey towards spiritual being, according to Howe. The 'mother' is a hollowed-out form, while the 'child' is a new life surging up within the hollow. By looking deeply into the hollow of this form, inhabited as it is by a new life, you can observe the effect of *kenosis*, that emptying of self or death which precedes all new life and rebirth. Without this emptying, there can be no death or transformation. 'The depth of our *spiritual being* somehow corresponds to the depth of our kenosis.'[3]

The very act of chipping away at the stone is integral to the whole process. Both the figure emerging along the way and the stone being removed are part of the sculpture. The passion with which the sculptor applies the hammer and chisel indicates his intimate implication in the medium. The closer the relationship between artist and art, says Howe, the more fully will the sculptor draw substance from the work and become one with it. In our own inner engagements, we draw our substance progressively from an increasingly intimate contact with the spiritual realities we encounter and become one with the journey. We are, in fact, the journey which empties self to receive new life.

All spiritual life is a journey arising from our innate capacity for God which is then awakened and developed through immersion in the mystery of Christ. This is facilitated by assimilating the Word of God, which can ultimately lead to a transformation of being. What, then, is born of the monastic is offered to the world. The capacity for God is 'the power and the glory', not only of the monk, but of every Christian and every human being. This need is the image of God in our depths which seeks its likeness, the fundamental dynamism of our being.

Born in Massachusetts, Howe studied at Columbia University, New York. In 1953 she entered the Trappistine Abbey of Notre-Dame de L'Assomption in Rogersville, New Brunswick. Named after a Roman Catholic bishop, the village lies in a constitutionally bilingual province in North Eastern Canada, close to the Atlantic Gateway, and is home to two monasteries – one for men, the other for women. Although her journey has been lived out in a monastic context, the insights of this cloistered nun about the growth of 'spiritual being' can be applied to all walks of Christian life. Spiritual being is a state of being that is in the process of continual yet imperceptible transformation.

Howe recalls a time, in early middle age, when she recognised a spiritual reality in the face of a spiritual mother. Her eyes were opened and she learnt to see. For several years it was that face which determined the journey because there was something in it that had touched her, awakened a consciousness within and propelled her pursuit. She began to identify the same countenance on the faces of others. The face became for her 'the locus of spiritual life' and helped form an inner vision as she immersed herself more and more in this world, which she saw as an immersion in the mystery of Christ.

Immersion is a way of being that can help us access that deeper life which is the ultimate meaning of all existence. All life, but especially monastic living, is an immersion into the mystery of Christ, an immersion of the substance of the person in the substance of the mystery: an interpenetration. Through baptism, which means immersion, we are all sacramentally immersed in the Christ mystery, the source of 'Spiritual Life'. Nuns and monks refer to their profession as a second baptism. In Cistercian life, immersion takes place at the physical level (the Rule, community, vows, asceticism, solitude and silence), the intellectual (the study of scripture, theological writings and monastic doctrine) and the spiritual (the life of the heart, prayer, lectio divina and liturgy). The goal of all three levels is an actual participation, the pure mystery of immersion in Christ.

Howe makes an important distinction between her analogies of immersion and swimming. Immersion is a sinking into, a letting go of self and just being, allowing the water to penetrate all the pores. Swimming is a visible, external action which does something as it goes towards a predetermined goal, choosing the means, observing the progress and being attentive to the results of our efforts. She indicates that we can swim in the spiritual life or be immersed in it. It is natural for monastics to immerse, as their way of living gives them access to a deeper life at the root of existence.

Immersion is not inactivity but makes radical and urgent demands. We can be immersed but remain impermeable. Think of a rock put into water, she says, it is one thing to be immersed but another to be adequately porous to absorb the reality into which we have been plunged. Yet permeability in the contemplative life is the crux of the matter. In order to be porous, letting the divine through, there has to be *kenosis* or self-emptying which is indispensable for depth and transformation. There is also the need for continuity. We have to remain in the water. 'Duration in our spiritual endeavour is one of the secrets of monastic life,' Howe reveals. 'It is the price we pay for depth and acuity in monastic life. If we make continual compromises or even become too taken up with activities, we pay for it in the long run by an increasing shallowness and dullness.'[4] Immersion, then, especially for monastics, is about remaining in the depths (even though we may not be conscious of them) and trusting that transformation will occur. The mystery of Christ is acting upon us in the monastery, she tells her fellow monastics, and we are responding to it. Too human an interpretation of what is happening might result in a state of being closed. This can manifest itself in such dispositions as bitterness, hardness of heart, fear, anger and ambition. These entrap us in ourselves and sever the interaction with the mystery. At the end of the day, the heart must be penetrated by Christ.

In the monastery, spiritual formation and guidance became Howe's special undertaking and she served as formation director for many years. Her own personal journey that was gathering momentum at this time provided the impetus for her work. Through her studies, the dynamic relationship of the image and likeness of God took hold and led her into a new understanding of the heart, a journey into an ever-deepening consciousness. If you wish to attain the heart of another, she says, it is from one's own heart that life must flow.

With a desire for the Absolute and a basic capacity for human truth, a spiritual mother is on her own journey, responding to a call from beyond, but she is also present to this world. If she is perceptive about human nature and personalities, she can meet people where they are and journey with them into the realities of the spiritual world with an awareness of the particular needs and affinities of each person. As a guide, the *amma* seeks to open the consciousness or awaken the heart to spiritual realities, *the sens intime*. It is an accompaniment into an immense new world as the other person is helped to see the realities of that experience, a vision received through the eyes of the heart. Once this sense of the spiritual unfolds, the eyes are sensitised to related realities wherever they be.

Howe likens this teaching to the difference between immersing ourselves in water and swimming on the surface. Immersion is essential and needs to be continual if our hearts (or substance) are to be emptied and opened so they can be penetrated by the mystery of Christ.

While the spiritual journey is always an adventure, involving our whole being and giving vitality to our entire life, we still need to be patient and attentive, 'suspended above the whole'. The quest is an answer to a call which becomes a wound for the Absolute, for Truth, for God: 'It is by this wound that what is most real in us awakens and sets out on the quest,' she writes. 'Prayer itself is a progressive ever-deepening wound opening into Christ's wound.' Sanctity, she adds, is a divine wound.[5]

When a spiritual mother agrees to travel with another person, she agrees to be changed by the other, Howe says. In her work of guiding others, she found that the use of symbols and images became catalysts. The 'Face' is about the progress from image to likeness. The 'River' relates to the underground river in us, the deepest level of spiritual life. The 'River of Water' is plenitude when we arrive at willing what God is willing. The 'River of Wine or Fire' is divinisation when we cannot *not* will what God wills. She also uses 'Reed' and 'Song' as metaphors. A person becomes more and more a reed as she is hollowed out by the spiritual life. The life that grows in her is a song that becomes increasingly divine.

After serving for many years as formation director at her monastery, Howe was elected abbess in 1978, a responsibility she held until her retirement twenty-one years later. During this time, she rediscovered the psalter and a method for entering into it. One day, as she began reading the psalms aloud to herself, softly and gently, she found herself listening to the words rather than merely repeating them.

Creating the impression of journey, she started tapping on the table slowly and regularly at the same time as she listened. Gradually she found herself 'walking into the psalms'. It was neither a meditation nor a reflection but a *moving into*. Each psalm began to reveal something through the words and yet beyond them. Much like the experience of the face many years before, she was being drawn into a deeper level of consciousness. She was able to share this with those she accompanied.

As we immerse ourselves in the psalms, she suggests, we should listen attentively for the unchanging bass, the 'I Am' which flows under the ever-changing melodies. Here the full mystery burns in a moment. 'Once a psalm is experienced, a pull, an irresistible attraction, makes itself felt, which causes one to leave everything, so to speak, and walk into the psalms,' she notes. 'Walking into the psalms is walking toward the heart.

Coming through the psalms is coming into the heart. Walking into the psalms is walking into the heart of Christ, into the heart of humanity, into our own heart.'[6]

But such a practice does not shield us from the suffering of the world to which we must respond. At the 'still point of the turning world', our hearts are in union with the heart of Christ, beating at the heart of the world. As we journey through prayer towards the Holy Trinity, the life that has taken root in us can grow 'even to the point of making us a holocaust'[7] through whom He blows, through whom He burns so that the words we speak and pray are those of fire. Spiritual guides are involved in a serious endeavour when they help to give birth to a life that can save and heal the world, even though the process and its fruits are likely to be unseen and unknown. 'Those in whom that life is born are wounded and cannot stop their journey,' she writes.[8]

Practising the Presence

Brother Lawrence, or Nicholas Herman of Lorraine (1611–91), served as a soldier and footman for a grand French family, where he annoyed his employers by breaking everything. Then, at the age of fifty-five, he entered the Carmelite Order in Paris as a lay brother and became a cook. Known as Brother Lawrence, he laid claim to no special gifts but felt God's presence constantly, whether working in the kitchen or worshipping in church. There was no distinction between a time of business and a time of formal prayer. Brother Lawrence's conversations and letters recording his communion with God were first published a year after his death. This suggests that his own presence made an impression on the community which recognised that the depth of his words could edify other Christian lives. These preservatives of spiritual wisdom were not left on the shelf and to this day, under the title *The Practice of the Presence of God*, continue to be a source of inspiration for those seeking and experiencing the divine in the midst of everyday life.[9]

In the book we learn how, at the age of eighteen, he undergoes a life-changing experience on a midwinter's day when he observes a dry and leafless tree standing gaunt against the snow. It is clearly a contemplative awakening that the bareness can be transformed. He feels an overwhelming sense of the knowledge and love of God, and makes it his business to walk as in his presence. The conversations and correspondence confirm that contemplation is not dependent on any form of theological scholarship but on an open heart to God at all times in a spirit of repentance, love and service. For Brother Lawrence, prayer is a continual conversation with God that goes on among the pots and the pans as much as it does kneeling before a tabernacle. He sees shame in stopping it because he might start to think of 'trifles and fooleries'.[10] The soul is insensible to everything except divine love. When the appointed times of prayer are over, his relationship with God does not suddenly end or change because he carries on praising and blessing in a state of joy. In the heat of kitchen life, he still manages to preserve his recollection and heavenly-mindedness as he prepares meals for his brothers. We read that he is never hasty or casual but maintains an even, uninterrupted composure and tranquillity of spirit. He comments: 'The time of business does not with me differ from the time of prayer, and in the noise and clutter of my kitchen, while several persons are at the same time calling for different things, I possess God in as great tranquillity as if I were upon my knees at the Blessed Sacrament.'[11]

Brother Lawrence understands the meaning of divine possession. He seeks to become 'wholly God's'. Sometimes he sees himself as a stone before a carver who would make a statue of him as 'His perfect image in my soul, and render me entirely like Himself'.[12]

He actually hopes God will 'give him somewhat to suffer'[13] so his spiritual life will grow stronger. He is living in an age that believes God sends diseases of the body to cure those of the soul. Like other mystics, he states that pain and suffering would be 'a Paradise to me, while I should suffer with my God'.[14] He also believes that if we grow accustomed to the exercise of the presence of God, our illnesses will be much alleviated.

Brother Lawrence counsels a correspondent not to use too many words or long discourses when praying because these cause the mind to wander. His guidance is to 'hold yourself in prayer before God like a dumb or paralytic beggar at a rich man's gate'.[15]

When I read that the kitchen contemplative sometimes considered himself 'before Him as a poor criminal at the feet of his judge',[16] I was reminded of the time I stayed in a monastic retreat house and was cooked meals by an oblate who told me that he had been jailed for armed robbery. In fact, Ralph had been in twenty-seven prisons and had even shot a gangster who torched his flat. A life of crime, alcoholism, cocaine and heroin addiction had been halted by a series of life-transforming experiences, including, he insisted, a visitation by the Archangel Michael.

It was by all accounts an extraordinary tale of how one man had been hollowed out by God and transformed in the process. As I was on a retreat, trying to forget my reporting life, I wasn't really in the mood for chatting to the guest house manager and I was certainly not expecting my journalistic curiosity to be aroused by him. But there in the middle of the Bedfordshire countryside, without any professional accoutrements, I found myself listening to one of the best stories I had ever heard: from the prison cell to the monastic cell. What was more, it had never been publicly told: an exclusive being presented to me on a plate in the most unlikely setting of a monastery kitchen. At that point Ralph did not know how I earned my bread. After I decided that I ought to disclose it, he became even more animated. I was especially intrigued to learn that, after listening in his cell one day to a service being broadcast by the BBC, he began to think about turning his life around. The programme was a catalyst for a spiritual conversion.

Ralph's journey had been a lifelong search for love and security. His father died before he was born. A twin, he was the only child in the family to be sent to an orphanage until he was ten. After going to sea as a teenager, he wed and had children but the marriage dissolved. His mother died in front of him as she was peeling potatoes. This all led Ralph to take to the bottle and live as a vagrant, drifting in and out of work. Then he turned to crime and spent fourteen years behind bars, eight of them for double armed robbery. In his mid forties, he robbed a rent office at gunpoint not once but twice in a fortnight. As an inmate, he was no stranger to the temptations of drugs, drink and pornography, but at the same time he looked to his own personal development, passing an A-level in English literature and undertaking a course in computer literacy.

Then, one New Year's Day, he underwent a series of life-changing experiences, including the visitation by the Archangel Michael. He had seen a figure in front of him and a strange light encompassed him. Visions and dreams involving the Blessed Virgin Mary and the Pope followed. He interpreted the apparitions as a call to religious conversion. After attending Catholic Mass in jail, he decided to abandon his nominal Anglican affiliation because he felt a sense of homecoming. Guided by the chaplain, he was received into the Roman Catholic Church. He read the Bible dutifully and enrolled on a catechetical course. As prompts to prayer, he filled his cell with glow-in-the-dark kitsch while inmates dubbed him 'the monk'. Faith was natural to him and he had a strong devotion to the eucharist and the Virgin Mary.

Then, from an anonymous source, he received a book in the post. It was entitled *Christ's Call to the Monastery*. So, with a keen sense of providence, as his release date drew near, he decided to write to abbots asking for jobs. As he had a small navy pension, all he desired was a room and a bowl of broth at the end of the day. Although many of the monasteries responded with caution, one agreed to take him on probation. When two brothers collected him from a café near the prison, they were surprised to find him smartly dressed in a black suit with his shorn hair like a tonsure.

Ralph did not expect the monastic environment to come as a shock. He knew how a small room could take on a special character and become a home. He longed, though, for a more caring community than a prison. He expected his new inmates to show love to him all the time and was disappointed when he found tensions among them too. It was a less structured place than many of the institutions he had experienced and some of the other monasteries around. At one level, though, Ralph could not stop seeing himself as a criminal. Once an opportunist thief stole money from the monastery and Ralph was wrongly convinced that suspicion would fall on him.

The venture was, however, a risk for the community. While Ralph was devoted to its prayer life and anxious to please everyone, he could be garrulous and melodramatic. The monks soon sensed he would be too loud for the monastery building itself so they asked him to take care of the guest house, which he kept scrupulously spick and span. But he needed a specific role and arranged for someone to make white smocks for him so he could be 'half a monk'. Despite his vulnerabilities and frailties, he stuck with his vocation, working with grace as it confronted him again and again. When told he had passed his probationary period and could stay in the monastery, Ralph danced around the room exclaiming: 'I've got a home! I've got a home!' His presence was enriching the community. He toned down his manner and the brothers observed a humility forming. He said he felt called by God to become a monk.

After my few days at the monastery, Ralph and I kept in touch a little by email as I pondered the best way of telling his story. However, unbeknown to me, in the months that followed, Ralph was starting to lose weight. One morning he woke up with stomach pains and looked jaundiced. Hospital tests following an emergency admission revealed he had terminal cancer, but this was not disclosed to Ralph, who had always been alarmed that he might one day receive such a diagnosis. He returned to the monastery where he learnt he had only a short time to live. The brothers recognised an authentic divine call in him to be professed a monk and agreed this would be fulfilled. Ralph fulfilled all the criteria in *The Rule of St Benedict* in terms of whether someone should be allowed to persevere in the monastic life. Ralph genuinely sought God, showed obedience, if at times with difficulty, was always faithful to the offices and could put up with harsh words, even though they were not always easily heard.

Ralph was home and dry. But with the days ticking by, he had to be fast-tracked. As he was short in stature, none of the brethren's habits would fit, so they had to borrow one from another monastery. The service of profession took place in the chapel but because he was so weak he had to make his life vows sitting in a chair. As part of the ritual, three times he had to say the words: 'Sustain me, Lord, according to your promise and I shall live.' In the circumstances, this was particularly poignant for those who were present. It was customary for a prospective monk to be a postulant for nine months and a novice for at least a year before making simple vows for three years and his solemn vows after that. Ralph completed the cycle in a day and was welcomed as Brother Michael.

He had only twelve days to live. Determined to have his own habit, Brother Michael asked the same person who had designed his white smocks to oblige with a garment he knew would cover his body at death. Although the illness had rapid physical and psychological consequences, the new monk struggled to the chapel to say his prayers and addressed his dying with remarkable dignity, courage and faith. And he still appreciated the theatre of it, bestowing blessings to visitors as they passed. But, even as his health was deteriorating, when he heard a report about a local bank robbery, he was still convinced that people would suspect him. It was important for him to know he was loved.

As the shadows lengthened, a hospice-trained nurse supervised the brother's last days. He continued to receive visitors but prayer became his primary focus, even though the practising of it was difficult. When he could no longer get to the chapel, he said the rosary from his bed and the brothers came and prayed with him. In the quiet atmosphere of his last day, Brother Michael was incapable of moving or responding much, so members of the community prayed at his bedside. As his breathing slowed to the sound of psalms being prayed around him, the newest member of the community passed away, less than a fortnight after his profession for life.

4

Awakening to Reality

It was a bleak Friday afternoon in a town in northern England where I was trying to live more contemplatively. The oppressive grey skies, not uncommon in that part of the world, were weighing down on the one-time mining community which had known more flourishing times. I had been to a supermarket to stock up on provisions. After putting the carrier bags into the boot, I selected an album from the car's music system. It was a recording by the Paris Gregorian Chant Choir. The traffic was slow and monotonous, and the depressed landscape kept me in a flat frame of mind. But as the singing began to envelop me in the driver's seat, I became aware, not of any dissonance between the music and the environment, but of their mysterious connection.

As I drove on, the chant seemed to permeate my entire being, lifting me into another realm. When I looked through the windows, I saw faces bathed in a new light. Ordinary scenes, like schoolchildren larking about in the street at the end of the school week or a grandmother correcting her charge, took on a different character. The mundane displayed a beauty I had never fully appreciated and, despite the dismal streets and skies, the chant seemed to induce an inner radiance through which I felt the interconnection of all people and all things, a unity at the heart of creation.

I remember something similar happening after I had been to a community of Hindu monks in Britain. In a characteristic act of kindness, one of the brothers gave me two packets of coconut biscuits for the journey home. An hour or so later, I was waiting for a connection at a busy railway station and decided to have a snack. As I opened the packet, I noticed a bird with a stump foot, hopping along the platform. I bent down to feed it with crumbs and noticed that it stayed close to me as the next train pulled in. I don't think any passengers even noticed what was going on but in the middle of a chaotic travelling situation, with cases and trolleys moving all around us, the bird and I struck up a relationship. It was almost as if the activity around me went out of focus as the spotlight turned on an incidental encounter which, to me, captured the way in which a contemplative approach to life leads to awareness or mindfulness. I sent a text to the monk to tell him how his hospitality had fed both a peckish journalist and a wounded bird. He sent a message back reminding me of the interconnectedness of all of creation and how I was seeing with the heart.

Monk-in-the-world Wayne Teasdale says nature constantly teaches us that a larger picture exists than what we see. It compels us to awaken by confronting us with order, design, and perfection everywhere. The inner gaze of attentiveness enabled Teasdale to see, experience and know the outer world in a deeper way. This is cultivated through deep attention to what is before us and by being receptive to the divine wherever we are. The divine presence awakens this capacity in us. What we might otherwise overlook or take for granted is brought to our notice.

> A spider weaving its web, the perfect symmetry of a snow-flake, the beauty and harmony of the lily, the cosmic quality of trees, the mysterious presence of the wind, the attraction of stillness, the radiance of light, the transparency of fragrances, the flow of water, the movement of leaves, the timeless feeling of some days and nights, the poetry of birds in flight, the transfiguring moments of dawn and sunset, the hypnotic rhythm of the tides – all speak to us of something beyond ourselves, something that transcends our understanding. All

point to nature's ability to nourish us aesthetically and psychologically as well as materially.[1]

Humanity is healed and renewed through some people because of their availability, their extreme attention to others and the alacrity with which they give themselves to Christ, according to the Romanian Orthodox theologian Father Dumitru Staniloae. He has harnessed the worlds of theology and spirituality to produce insights on prayer of remarkable depth. His work enables us to understand more clearly the connections between contemplation and ministry, underscoring what it means to become the presence of God in the world. His thinking on saintliness inspires all who pray and minister to be expansive in their holy loving. 'The saint shows us a bearing full of tact, transparency, purity of thought and feeling, in relation to every human being,' Staniloae writes. 'His consideration extends even to animals and to things, because in every creature he sees a gift of God's love, and does not wish to wound that love by treating his gifts with negligence or indifference. He has respect for each man and for each thing. He shows towards the suffering of any man, or even of an animal, a profound compassion.'[2]

These words mirror those of St Isaac the Syrian who speaks of the compassionate heart as one which burns with love for every creature: human beings, birds, animals; for serpents and for demons. The thought and sight of them make tears flow. This immense and intense compassion, flowing from the heart, makes saints unable to bear the sight of the most insignificant wound in any creature. So they pray ceaselessly and with tears for animals, enemies of the truth and those who do them wrong.

Such compassion, says Staniloae, reveals a heart that is tender, extremely sensitive and a stranger to all hardness, indifference and brutality. It shows us that hardness is the result of sin and of the passions. In the bearing of the saints, and even in their thoughts, there is no trace of vulgarity, meanness or baseness, no sign of affectation or lack of sincerity. In the saints, kindliness, sensitivity and transparency come to their fullest expression and are combined with purity, generous attention to others and the availability by which they share fully in the problems and troubles of another. In all these qualities, the full capacity of human nature flowers and can encourage those of us who care for others to embrace tenderness and holiness in one act of self-giving.

Protecting Our Gifts

At his inaugural Mass in Vatican City on the solemnity of St Joseph in March 2013, Pope Francis spoke of the human vocation to be a protector in the world. This is another way of articulating what it means to become the presence of God to others. Referring to the mission that God entrusted Joseph to be the *custos* or protector of Mary, Jesus and by extension the mystical body known as the church, he said that every human being shared in this calling to be a protector. This implied protecting all creation, especially the beauty of the created world, as the Book of Genesis had told us and to which St Francis of Assisi had witnessed. It involved respecting each of God's creatures and the environment in which we live together. It commanded us to protect people by showing loving concern for every member of the human race, particularly children, the elderly and others in need, 'who are often the last we think about'. It entailed caring for one another in our families if we were parents, and protecting our mothers and fathers when they grew older. The Pope went on:

> It means building sincere friendships in which we protect one another in trust, respect and goodness. In the end, everything has been entrusted to our protection and all of us are responsible for it. Be protectors of God's gifts!
> Whenever human beings fail to live up to this responsibility, whenever we fail to care for creation, and for our brothers

and sisters, the way is opened for destruction and our hearts are hardened. Tragically, in every period of history there are 'Herods' who plot death, wreak havoc and mar the countenance of men and women.

Please, I would like to ask all those who have positions of responsibility in economic, political and social life, and all men and women of goodwill: let us be 'protectors' of creation, protectors of God's plan inscribed in nature, protectors of one another and of the environment. Let us not allow omens of destruction and death to accompany the advance of this world! But to be 'protectors', we also have to keep watch over ourselves. Let us not forget that hatred, envy and pride defile our lives! Being protectors, then, also means keeping watch over our emotions, over our hearts, because they are the seat of good and evil intentions: intentions which build up and tear down! We must not be afraid of goodness or even tenderness.

It is clear from the Pope's words that caring for the earth is a duty we all share as contemplatives in the world. In the same manner, Teasdale says that when he reflected on the natural world and 'its glorious message for us', he remembered our responsibility to restore and preserve it, to work towards a sustainable future in which the human community lived in harmony with nature. 'We have a sacred duty to the earth itself, to one another, and to all the other species that inhabit our planet, to live in a state of friendship with the natural world, enhancing its life by simplifying our needs and desires.'[3]

Teasdale also writes that awareness fosters our understanding of the interconnectedness of all beings. It allows us to understand that justice cannot be defined or implemented without taking into account the interdependence of all beings. We become the presence of God, then, not only to our fellow human beings but also to our kindred creatures. This makes us sensitive to suffering in all its guises, including that endured by animals and birds. I remember finding a pigeon crushed by a horse and cart just outside the gates to Central Park in New York. Like the encounter on the railway platform, no one seemed to notice as I discreetly went over to the body, wrapped it in a scarf and took it to a resting place under leaves in a corner of the park, saying prayers as I carried it in a private procession to its burial spot. Whenever it has not been clearly dangerous or obviously unhygienic, I have also carried out these impromptu funeral rites for roadside rabbits, badgers and even once for a fox apparently shot in the face by a farmer.

A New Resurrection

Time spent in a monastic setting can cultivate this sense of awareness if we are open to it. When I visited a small suburban monastery during Advent, the abbess and the community were singing the *Rorate caeli* – 'May dew descend from heaven' – during the midday office. Mother Paula pointed out to me afterwards that we are dependent both for our earthly and spiritual lives on water, as well as the grace of God and the life that it presents. As the sisters were singing the antiphon they were asking for more abundant life, sometimes upon the parched earth and sometimes upon a parched soul. It was a present longing which could be experienced every day of our lives. 'In order to appreciate a feast, you have to fast,' said Mother Paula. 'If you have too much all the time, when good things come you scarcely notice them.' Benedictines are taught to see creation as the good gift entrusted to humanity to cherish and sustain. The world is sacramental, touched by God, and capable of revealing Him.

After a monastic dinner eaten in silence, Mother Paula took me on a tour of the grounds. The earth was still frozen hard. Some people dread winter in the northern hemisphere because of its limited natural light, but Mother Paula said she wished there were less artificial illumination so that we could 'once again be enfolded in the darkness' and see the sky and the stars more clearly. We could then identify even more with the people we were, longing for the dawn of day and for the breaking of the light. We could then learn to rejoice in the light instead of taking it for granted.

'Many people are frightened of the dark and they panic, in the same way as many people are frightened of silence because they don't want to find out what is inside themselves and they will do anything to block it out,' said Mother Paula. 'But anyone who has been able to enter into a certain silence and into a certain darkness – after the particular demons that we all seem to have in our minds have been driven out, mostly through prayer – discovers that darkness is creative. After all, a baby in the womb comes into being through darkness and seeds in the soil come to being in darkness. This is why Advent is the most creative time of year. The darkness is not a shell, because that is hard, but an enfolding darkness, a warm, creative darkness, the cover for our own being to become truly itself and then gradually burst out through this and grow.

'It is a form of allowing our being to increase in capacity and then it has to break through, root and thrust forth like a seedling and come into the light. Advent is a wonderful season. But I think too many people are afraid of it.'

As she had drawn my attention to various plants, Mother Paula spoke of creation itself as being a complete cycle. It began in the evening, moved into night and then day. 'In a way we are born so as to enter into darkness in order for it to become a new resurrection or, as we say in German, *eine neue Auferstehung*. Every time the sun rises, you have this new birth which we participate in as the day dawns. One can hear again birds singing, life and hope and joy. The whole Christian year, as it has been inserted into the natural year, is in fact making use of all the opportunities, which the seasons provide us with, so we can grow in the knowledge and love of God. We are also given a sense that we ourselves are constantly being allowed to grow, to change, to die, to go into a right space and to go into a wider space.

'I was pondering on *The Parable of the Sower* recently. There is nothing wrong with the sower, who is doing his work correctly, and there is nothing wrong with the seed. But there is quite a lot wrong with the field which is a hard path, a rocky path but there are also the fertile areas. It came to me that, if *we* are the field, we cannot till ourselves and break ourselves up. So how do we do this? It has to be by what happens to us in our life. There will be certain times when we are broken open by sorrow, grief, despair and all the other human emotions which can tear us apart. If we allow tears and compassion to enter us as well, there will be some soil and we know that we need something. We can then allow a seed to enter our being, a seed of hope. If we do not experience the pains of life, we are likely to remain rather hard and very unreal. Furthermore, we are not going to be people who are happy in ourselves because we are hard. We are not going to be really very much use to anybody else because we haven't been broken open sufficiently to allow our humanity to come forth.

'We are always aware of everything being renewed from a time of chaos, pain and suffering in the world. Yet if one looks at the soil – and the soil of one's own being – there's always new life there coming out of chaos. Chaos seems so important together with darkness.'

Mother Paula said Benedictines looked forward in Advent to the birth of Christ and a New Creation which would 'also be our own new creation in the heart of God'. Penitential practices, in Advent and Lent, would have no value at all if the community was not looking forward in hope to something better, for a greater fullness of life. Waiting was a state of being. This meant that any impatience and desire for instant gratification had to be cast away.

'When we wait, we can look around us and see what is there. We can appreciate the present moment and we can, for a time at least, be present to the here and now. That is a value in its own right. We wait because we are hoping for something. If we had nothing to hope for, then this could be a time for despair. But, even then, the waiting can still put us in touch to a greater degree both with God and with our human situation. It also helps us to learn to appreciate what is – not what was, or what will be, but what is. So I think waiting is a most wonderful gift.

'Without the waiting, the fasting, and the doing without, we cannot really appreciate the gift that is given. Even in the monastic life, there are times when we are given too much. So often we say thank you to people and wonder what on earth we can do with these things that we don't need and don't want. How can we pass them on to others who could need them? So we have entered into a cycle of recycling so that the gift – yes we have appreciated it – is passed on to the poor or missions so that it spreads out further and not just to us who do not need it.'

Mother Paula explained that pointing people back to the truths had to come through their humanity and not any specifically religious guise. Sometimes the best evangelisation took place when a sister in her habit was in the waiting room of a hospital (an example of becoming the presence of God). People often started talking to the nun because they were nervous and frightened. 'I think we just enjoy the humanity of other people. It's not a question of what their religion is or isn't, but that they are human beings. So often these people, who apparently have no religion, are very much concerned for other people. They are not selfishly trying to get things for themselves and their family but have a real outreach to others. This is most heartening. Although secular society may not be very aware of God and may even be contemptuous about God, people are, in fact, aware that they are called to do good for other people. In *The Parable of the Last Judgement* in St Matthew's Gospel, it isn't the people who know God who are being praised for their good work but those, in fact, who do not know they are doing any good, particularly for God. But they are doing it for other people. So the real questions are: How are we treating each other? How are we treating creation? It would seem that God accepts any action – for good or bad – as given to *Him*. As he receives the good, he also receives the bad from our hands, and from our hearts and our minds.'

By now we had reached a patch of the garden where the four seasons seemed to have come together. Carpets of violets had spread across one corner. Some seeds put down for birds and squirrels had planted and would grow. Nasturtiums from the summer were still in flower, while close by were the wet autumn leaves from the beech trees and horse chestnuts. Advent was a new beginning and the leaves symbolised both the end of a year and new growth. Nature needed a rest period. 'I used to think that, when I was distracted, my thoughts were like leaves tumbling down from the trees,' Mother Paula recalled. 'Then I remembered that they decay and renew the soil, so that every-thing, even thoughts I don't like, can in fact be an enrichment of my own being. From there, new things can grow so the earth, soil and just natural beauty are tremendously important for understanding our spiritual lives. For those of us who are still able to walk in the garden and in the enclosure, it's a bit like being in Eden and seeing everything with fresh eyes.'

The Eternal Freshness of God

Another monastic from whom I learned about the eternal freshness of God had spent some years as a hermit and felt closely in touch with natural beauty. Dame Maria Boulding, a Benedictine nun at Stanbrook Abbey in Worcestershire, was a scholar and writer, rooted in scripture and the works of St Augustine. We also met in Advent. She told me that the four weeks before Christmas represented 'the long, long wait of humanity' for the coming of Christ, the light of the world. We were getting near the end of the waiting time, not only the waiting of Israel in the Old Testament but also the waiting of all humanity now for Christ, the light of the world and, indeed, the waiting of the whole human race for His second coming, 'whatever that means'. The story of humanity was 'going somewhere, towards God's destiny for us'. The lit candles on the Advent wreath were lights of hope, waiting for Christ, waiting for God, the Light, to come into a very dark world.

Using texts of scripture, especially the psalms in which the longings of the people of God from centuries before Christ were articulated in poetic forms, the liturgy looked forward to this coming of the light. What struck her every year was the beauty of this mystery expressed through song. 'This comes fresh,' she enthused. 'It is the extreme freshness of God. You can sing or read the same texts, hear them again, year after year, and somehow they come fresh.' There was also the beauty of winter itself, when in darkness the stars appeared strong and vivid. It reminded her of the celebrations of the midwinter solstice, the rebirth of the sun in the middle of the northern darkness in northern Europe. What those ancients were groping for, Christianity came to answer.

At the time, Maria Boulding had been in the community for just over fifty-eight years. She had arrived one autumn day in 1947. 'It's very hard to say why I came really,' she told me. 'I think for most monks and nuns the reason you come is not the same as the reason you stay. People come for all sorts of strange reasons really, attracted by something or other, but you soon find out that whatever that something or other was is not going to see you through a lifetime. So you have to rethink your motives a good deal. In a very broad way, I suppose one can say it's a response to the love of God that one has known in one's life somehow.

'God makes himself known in *every* person's life somehow or other. Some of us follow that love that calls in this monastic way. It's only one way among a myriad of others of living out the response to God in Christ, living out our baptism.' According to Dame Maria, the experience of God worked itself out in many diverse ways – in beauty, human relationships, suffering, in moments of surprise and in the unexpected generosity of people, who sometimes were like 'touches of God' on our lives.

Reflecting on her own monastic journey, Dame Maria went on: 'One makes mistakes the whole time, not only at the beginning as a novice. You fall flat on your face over and over and over again. This is quite normal. One of the things about community life is that we carry each other in some kind of way. St Benedict talks near the end of the Rule about bearing one another's weaknesses and there is a real sense that there is room to make mistakes and fail. That's all right within the community. It's the context in which one can. That's great. This is not peculiar to monastics, of course, it's everywhere, in families and all sorts of things. A loving environment is an environment in which you can make mistakes and learn from them.

But contemplative life was not confined to monasteries. People tended to think it was some peculiar thing that monks and nuns got up to, but it was actually a normal fulfilment of Christian life, especially for anyone who lives a life of faith and prayer in Christ and ponders the mysteries. 'The contemplative life is *everybody's* business, not just monks and nuns,' she insisted. 'Monastics are living in a kind of life which does facilitate it – or should. In the sense that it's institutionalised in monasteries is marginal, I think. That's okay because marginality has a function in any human set up I think. The prophets of Israel, like Jeremiah, were a bit like that, standing a little outside the ordinary run of human life at the time. But that was important. It was a sign intended by God to point to what he wanted to point to.'

We were all called by God in Christ and were much more closely related to one another than we imagined, organically related or as St Paul put it 'equivalent'. There was a closeness to Christ and to one another in Christ. Contemplation was not about 'floating around on Cloud Nine'. For much of the time it was a hard slog through the desert – aloneness, struggle, barrenness and poverty, having nothing but God's mercy and God's will. Contemplative life was about slogging on in faith, in darkness, in the desert for much or even most of the time, but 'that was classic'. The desert was a definite part of the chosen people's life and had always been in the church, since Jesus himself chose to go into the desert for a key period in his life.

Dame Maria said there was a real call or even duty to integrate spirituality with the intellectual life. Christ had said: 'Thou shalt love the Lord thy God with thy whole heart, thy whole soul and thy own mind and thy whole strength.' This meant the whole person. A person had to grapple with that and find the best way to integrate it in oneself. Forming a unity in oneself was part of the job of anyone who was seriously living a life of prayer and who also had intellectual formation. There was an old monastic saying, *contemplata aliis tradere* – 'to hand on the results or fruits of contemplation' – which could mean many different things.

Although Advent had formed an indispensable part of her spiritual journey, Easter has underpinned Dame Maria's entire monastic life. She was clothed (received the habit) in Easter week 1948, made her first vows the same time a year later and her life vows in Easter week 1952. This had felt like a gift from God. Her vocation seemed connected with the paschal mystery of the Lord's death and resurrection. This was the main feature of the church's life, of every Christian's life, but of it Dame Maria said, 'I just feel it's been stamped on mine in a special way.' The liturgy, the whole cycle – the repetitive celebration of Christ's mysteries of redemption, from his birth, through to his public life, suffering, death, resurrection, glorification, sending of the Spirit – unfolded in a sequence through the year but, because it mostly developed in the northern hemisphere, it sang along or chimed in with our natural cycles from Advent to Harvest.

'I have terrific pleasure out of the changing colours of the trees in autumn, the appearance of certain buds in the spring or looking at the first snowdrops – which gets earlier and earlier,' she said. 'It used to be February, now it's January and even back in December because we get warmer and warmer, which I don't like. I love animals and they give me immense joy if I get in touch with them in any way, birds or whatever. This becomes more intense or fresh somehow as I get older and live life longer.'

Among Maria Boulding's books is found an exploration of failure.[4] In a success-orientated culture, failure is being written off, she writes. You fail and that is it. But there is room in Christian life for failing. Jesus himself in a *certain* sense did fail. If he had been looking for a marvellous career of preaching, healing and teaching, it was cut very short. He failed; and all his little band that he had been gathering so carefully and preparing so carefully all took to their heels and scarpered. Jesus was left alone. He fell apart in a terrible way. We tend to read the story backwards because we know that he is going to rise again on Easter Sunday. But, from his vantage point as a human being, it cannot have looked like that. In his human mind he must have felt that he had failed. It is a terrible disaster at one level, but the whole point of the story is that disaster and failure were in God's infinite plan – the way in which Jesus was going to redeem our failed world and, of course, did.

So failure can be used constructively and creatively in human life if we unite it with the Cross. The Jesuit poet Gerard Manley Hopkins recognised the mess we make of the world and how we smear it, spoil it and make it dirty. There is always, though, this freshness, this 'deep down thing', the Holy Spirit. 'Certainly we're promised a new heaven and a new earth whatever that may mean,' she told me. 'Scripture says so but we don't know what it means. But we can think about it this way I think: Christ's risen body, Christ's risen human body and human mind are like the explosive, radioactive nucleus of the new world, the new creation: that *all creation* is already being redeemed in Him and will in the end be glorious in Him. St Paul talks about it all groaning in travail and giving birth. We haven't seen that new birth as yet but we see little bits of it, I think. Teilhard de Chardin was a prophet in some sort of way. I think he saw a great deal and did understand a lot about this creation of the new world – and not only as some unimaginable distant thing, but something we can contribute to now by our lives and our work, and the way we honour beauty and so on.'

Searching and finding were all of a piece on the inner journey, said Dame Maria. God was supposed to have said to Pascal: 'You would not be seeking me unless you had already found me.' She believed this was true for all of us. St Benedict said in the Rule about a newcomer being examined to discover if he were really seeking God, or some other end instead. God was 'infinitely beyond us, *infinitely* beyond us'. She added: 'We'll never come to the end of God or think we've got him sorted out and taped. It's not like that. Even in heaven, presumably, when we see Him face to face, I suppose we go on seeking. I don't know. St Augustine ventures to say he thinks possibly we do, so I'm in good company. But you seek and you find, and you find and you seek. And you never come to the end of God.'

A few years after our meeting, Maria Boulding died from cancer in the community's new eco-friendly monastery in North Yorkshire. She had anticipated that the final part of her earthly journey would be marked by thanksgiving and not interrupted so starkly by a terminal diagnosis. Letting go of her cherished independence, she learned to rely on all those who cared for her, though God remained in charge. It became a time of grace and discovery as she was awakened to the love of others, coming to believe in it, 'like a helpless child who has nothing to give except its need'.[5] As she faced her own death, Dame Maria wrote: 'Everyone who perseveres through the inner journey of prayer will have to let go of his or her ideas about how the journey should work out, and accept another, far more baffling, itinerary.'[6]

That was certainly my experience, as ordination led me on a completely different journey from the one I had imagined.

5

Contemplatives or Clerics?

Many have recognised that the church needs to recover its contemplative roots, which are so frequently smothered by the tentacles of clericalism – that model of haughty and aloof ministry which prizes spiritual power and superiority over humility and compassion to one's neighbour. This is one of the most dangerous obstacles to becoming the presence of God for others, because clericalised ministers (lay or ordained) place *themselves* at the centre of things and conceal their own shortcomings. Contemplatives, who put God and other people first, are always learners, in touch with their own humanity and failings.

Even back in the 1980s, the influential theologian and priest, Henri J.M. Nouwen, was making the case for a new form of Christian leadership, whose hallmarks would be contemplation and vulnerability. At a time when the church was speaking about the need to become more relevant to society, Nouwen was arguing precisely the opposite. In his reflections on Christian leadership, *In the Name of Jesus*, informed by his experience among people with developmental disabilities at L'Arche, Nouwen does not mince his words: 'The leader of the future will be the one who dares to claim his irrelevance in the contemporary world as a divine vocation that allows him or her to enter into a deep solidarity with the anguish underlying all the glitter of success and to bring the light of Jesus there.'[1] It is an irrelevance with nothing to offer but the minister's own vulnerable self. This is the way Jesus came to reveal God's love. God loves us not because of what we do or accomplish, but because God has created and redeemed us in love, and has chosen us to proclaim that love as the true source of all human life.

According to Nouwen, it is through contemplative prayer that overworked ministers prevent themselves from becoming strangers to their own hearts as well as the heart of God. Nouwen says the central question for them should not revolve around morality but around communion: how to be one with God? Ministers should be people 'with an ardent desire to dwell in God's presence, to listen to God's voice, to look at God's beauty, to touch God's incarnate word and to taste fully God's infinite goodness'.[2] For Christian leadership to be truly fruitful, there has to be a movement from the moral to the mystical. Christian leadership should not be about ministers wearing themselves out by worrying about the moral aspect of theology, but should motivate them to find new life by reclaiming its mystical dimension: union with God in prayer.

The mystery of ministry is that women and men have been chosen to make their own limited and conditional love the gateway for the unlimited and unconditional love of God. When the members of a community of faith cannot truly know and love their shepherd, shepherding can become a way of exercising power over others in an authoritarian way. The world in which we live – one of efficiency and control – has no models to offer those who want to be shepherds in the way Jesus was a shepherd. His was a servant leadership, in which the leader is a vulnerable servant who needs the people as much as they need him or her. So leadership should not be influenced by the power games of the world, but by Jesus, who came to give his life for the salvation of many.

In another text, Nouwen says he has been overwhelmed by the number of people who have been wounded by religion.[3] He states:

The most insidious, divisive, and wounding power is the power used in the service of God. An unfriendly word by a minister or priest, a critical remark in church about a certain lifestyle, a refusal to welcome people at the table, an absence during an illness or death, and countless other hurts often remain longer in people's memories than other more world-like rejections. Thousands of separated and divorced men and women, numerous gay and lesbian people, and all of the homeless people who felt unwelcome in the houses of worship of their brothers and sisters in the human family have turned away from God because they experienced the use of power when they expected an expression of love.[4]

One priest who has lived out Nouwen's theology is Father Luke Penkett, who ministers in an Anglican church in Hampshire. He was formerly an Orthodox priest-monk who lived as a solitary on the island of Guernsey. Father Luke is registered blind and has worked with the L'Arche community in England. He believes there are several lessons which L'Arche could teach the Christian leader in the early part of the twenty-first century, especially in Western society with its emphasis on the individual, immediacy and influence.

All assistants in L'Arche have an accompanier or spiritual supervisor. Early in his ministry there, Father Luke was told by his *accompagnateur* (Father David Standley, a Roman Catholic priest with many years' experience of the community) to 'focus on what you receive rather than trying to control'. Church leaders who focus on control, rather than what they receive, are often the ones who end up burning out while their congregations get smaller. 'When I look at churches where congregations have in fact dwindled to the faithful few, very often I go on to discover that their leaders have focused on control rather than what they receive,' he told me. 'They tend to have five, seven, or even more parishes in their so-called care. Parishioners who have been censured rather than welcomed no longer worship there.

'How can any Christian leader, beset by a vicious circle of so much compulsive emailing, so many urgent telephone messages, and a never-ending stream of erratic people needing immediate help, preserve some distance from – if not actually remain detached from – the worst aspects of Western society? I think at least part of the answer may be found in contemplative prayer.'

Father Luke came to experience L'Arche as a profoundly spiritual community, especially through the abiding awareness of the presence of God that he came to recognise in each person there. 'I discovered that L'Arche is a way of life and even, perhaps paradoxically, a contemplative one,' he said. 'Others have discovered this too – a spirit of unceasing prayer, attention to the present moment, patient waiting and healing. If a person tries to take over, it doesn't work at L'Arche, especially where spiritual matters are concerned. The more that person rushes around, anxiously trying to affirm others or seeking their affirmation, the further that person places themselves from God and from those being served. Rigid timetables are out of place in L'Arche. There is a mutuality of care there that can prevent this from happening – if there is wise and careful leadership.

'Sadly, there have always been, and always will be, assistants – and leaders too – in L'Arche who seek to control, who come with their own agenda, or who are blinded by the overprotective parents of core members, persons with learning disabilities. But, hopefully, they soon discover they are not accepted by the core members and are a cause of friction. They soon burn out or leave before they do too much damage.'

Father Luke says that, during his ministry at L'Arche, he was 'enabled to pray more, to be quieter, to be calmer and to discover God in my heart in ways that had not happened before. I was enabled to be in community. Above all, I was enabled to be more fully myself, to explore and accept more deeply my own disability, to learn from all my friends and to receive love, not for what I did, but for who I was.

'Contemplative prayer goes deeper than words and, in my experience, when there were problems of communication, prayer itself was intensified. It is so often the eyes of the person with communication problems which express so much. They are frequently far more eloquent than any words.'

For Father Luke, the move to L'Arche was, at first, challenging and tiring. He had always found that talking and writing flowed from him naturally. In the community, during the nightly prayer times together, he had to couch what he wanted to say in words that were understandable but not dumbed down. He knew the community would see through him if he did not express himself accordingly. He admits his first eucharistic service was far too wordy. What he had enjoyed doing before – being in control of the service – was no longer an option. Father Luke explained: 'My suggestions for the celebrating Triduum – the services of Maundy Thursday, Good Friday and the Easter Vigil – were, quite rightly, batted straight out of court and what replaced these, from other peoples' experiences of worshipping in L'Arche, was something far more spontaneous and fecund. I found the service of foot-washing on Maundy Thursday, where we all take it in turns to wash one another's feet (or hands), and the Good Friday service of the Cross, especially moving.'

In glimpsing the eternal, Father Luke pointed out, the contemplative is the person aware of the divine presence in others, who waits on others, who no longer needs, someone not hungry for human contact but guided by a vision of what he has seen beyond the immediate concerns of the world. 'But the blindfold that prevents us from seeing all of this has so often become an invisible one. This is because the theology that so many Christian leaders have developed and come to respect is one of health, wealth and success which reflect the values of our culture. The contemplative strips away the illusory blindfold of the present world, sees the truth of a situation and offers signs of hope.'

The ministry of the contemplative leader, who co-operates with God, will be different for each person, said Father Luke. Christian leaders need to let go of their power, their attempts to control and their search for success. Until they empty themselves of all that is worldly and embrace servanthood, they will burn out and misuse the authority placed in them. He went on: 'Until the church, the body of Christ, stops ascribing status to the wealthy rather than the poor, the powerful rather than those without power, the enabled rather than the disabled, it will continue to reject the significance of our status in Christ. Too often the church turns to the secular "wisdom" of society to discover a pragmatic solution to its problems and takes its lead from there. But an experience of L'Arche can inspire Christian leaders to help, share, support and trust, rather than disable, control and dominate. In a society that has moved from shutting away the disabled, to accepting and then learning from them, this is where hope lies for the church.'

A number of important writers have drawn attention to the failings of institutional religion and the damage it can cause. In a book chapter entitled 'Jesus and the Evil of Religion',[5] the psychotherapist Professor Brian Thorne says religion can be a most destructive force in the life of human souls, especially when, in their lust for power, ecclesiastical institutions or their representatives seek to preserve their absolute authority. This craving lends itself to 'an unscrupulous authoritarianism which cannot bear the uniqueness of persons and which beneath a cloak of virtue seeks to destroy those who by their inner security threaten its domination.'[6] Thorne cites Jesus at his trial, utterly secure in his own identity and unable to be touched at the core of his being by the false accusations of the religious leaders. It was *this* that infuriated them.

Contemplatives have not fallen silent on the issue. The Trappist writer, Thomas Keating, says if people would put their minds on becoming God – not in the sense of power but in serving every living thing as far as they have the strength and talents to do so – the world would become the Garden of Eden. Indeed, we have to make it Eden, 'or we will make it into a kind of hell'.[7] He points out that some believers have been so damaged by religious misinformation or malformation that they can no longer travel by that path. But for him 'God is sheer freedom, liberation, and this total freedom is the disposition that we are being invited into, so that we can be God, too, without pride or attributing anything to ourselves'.[8]

Wayne Teasdale chose to be an urban monk living in the heart of pulsating Chicago. Anchored in a deep and growing inner awareness of God's presence, he often felt 'the Divine One giving itself to me directly, in my relationships with others and in the natural world; it is always a source of inspiration, delight, and even bliss. I experience, and so am aware of this Presence, in some way, all the time.'[9] But after a series of visits to India, Teasdale began to understand spiritual experience differently. Captivated by the country's contemplative spirit, he started to relinquish his reliance on external structures and, more especially, his attitude to the church changed over time. His idealised vision evaporated; the security, peace, and comfort of the past were replaced by uncertainty, anxiety, and discomfort: 'Although I still loved the Church, I began to see the institution for what it was – divine in origin, as my faith and the tradition hold, but composed of frail human beings with their own motives, at different stages of spiritual attainment. I realised very simply that individuals who come to positions of power in the Church, but who are not very enlightened, can do enormous damage. Usually, this damage is political and moral.'[10]

A Roman Catholic priest-writer, who became the first ecclesial hermit in the United States, has also weighed in. A Discalced Carmelite (one who doesn't wear shoes), William McNamara, founded the Spiritual Life Institute which establish-ed a number of communities of apostolic hermits, including several in America and another in Ireland. 'Jesus didn't want rhapsodic fans, but intrepid, inventive followers,' he says.[11] McNamara claims countless Christians have left the church because they were 'not being nourished on the contemplative bread of the Mystical Body of Christ, on the Spirit, but were being regulated by the rules and roles of religion.'[12] We will never see God, he maintains, as long as we refuse to stop, take time, enter into holy leisure and contemplate:

> We will miss God in the busy hustle and bustle of our loquacious liturgies. We will miss God in our hurried, routinized, self-centred prayer. We will miss God in our frenzied activities. We will miss God above all in our education, whose goal is supposed to be contemplation according to Plato, Socrates, Aristotle, the Fathers of the Church, Thomas Aquinas, and any ancient or modern educator worthy of our attention. Without mystical vision, our education is a farce, our civilization a sham, religion an opium, liturgy a corpse, theology a fad, and apostolic outreach the most popular and pietistic escape from the God who said, 'Be still and see that I am God' (Ps 46:11).[13]

All of us could be archetypal monks, says McNamara. There is a need for more women and men to enter, interpret and manage 'the desert'. This would require an attitude and disposition where God is at the centre with each of us longing and yearning to be alone with him. Mystics discover through contemplation – a personal encounter with the living God – that they know nothing about God. They know not *what*, but only *that*, God is.

What Teasdale and McNamara reveal is the dichotomy that can clearly be drawn between the contemplative and the clerical. In my life of faith and in my work as a journalist, I have observed this division time and again. Of course, not every contemplative is virtuous and approachable, while not every priest is eaten up with envy and ambition; but, in general, one world seems focused on the spiritual and the other consumed by the religious. Clerics promoted up the ecclesiastical ladder do not necessarily get closer to God.

The Pope and the Prophets

In 2014, an Irish movie called *Calvary* hit the big screen.[14] Starring Brendan Gleeson as a Catholic priest who cares intensely for his flock, it follows an unsettling week in the prelate's life after being told by a parishioner during confession that he will be killed on a beach the following weekend. This unnerving prediction is not in retaliation for anything the grey-bearded prelate has done but because the 'penitent' was repeatedly abused as a child by a priest long dead. Like Christ himself, a good man must die for the sins of others.

While this dark film suggests that the catalogue of clerical abuse in Ireland and elsewhere should not imply most priests are corrupt, at the same time it shows how good men in the priesthood can be unfairly treated by parishioners because of the actions of other clerics.

Sexual abuse, though, is only one way in which some priests have betrayed the church. This was made evident by Pope Francis when, during his first year in office, he prayed publicly: 'Lord, free your people from a spirit of clericalism and aid them with a spirit of prophecy.' Pope Francis did not hesitate to denounce priests obsessed with spiritual power. In one of his daily homilies, preached at the St Martha guest house chapel in Rome, he said prophets were needed in the church to prevent a negative spirit of legalism from clouding the horizon.

'May our prayer in these days, during which we prepare for the birth of the Lord, be: "Lord, let there not be a lack of prophets among your people."'

A prophetic instinct is always part of becoming the presence of God because it sees things as they really are and isn't afraid of interpreting the signs of the times, however unpalatable. In contrast to the prophets, clerics of whatever denomination tend to be insecure people who sometimes control and oppress others because they are products of a controlling and oppressive system. They can be envious and resentful types. While prophets open up to the light, clerics close down, often operating in secrecy. They thrive on masks and blindfolds.

The Pope swiftly identified the clerics at the Vatican. He said that, in the gospel, those who met Christ with a spirit of prophecy welcomed him as the Messiah, but without it 'the void that is left is occupied by clericalism; and it is this clericalism that asks Jesus, "By what authority do you do these things? By what law?"' In the face of such scrutiny, the Pope said that the memory of the promise and the hope of going forward were reduced to the question of whether or not the present was 'legal'. The Pharisees who questioned the authority of Christ had not understood the prophecies. They had forgotten the promise. They did not know how to read the signs of the times; they had neither penetrating sight nor a hearing of the Word of God. They had only authority. But a prophet was someone who had in his heart the promise of God which he lived, remembered and repeated. The Lord, the pontiff said, had always safeguarded his people with the prophets – in difficult moments, in times in which the people were discouraged or destroyed, when the Temple was absent, when Jerusalem was under the power of the enemy and when the people wondered to themselves: 'But Lord, you promised us this! Now what happens?' In the heart of a prophet lay 'the promise of the past, contemplation of the present and courage to show the way towards the future'. A prophet was a person who reminded the people of God to move beyond a spirit of legality.

Maggie Ross, whose book *Pillars of Flame* is a damning indictment of clerical power,[15] told me candidates 'called to ministry' may, consciously or otherwise, actually be seeking power (out of a sense of inferiority), preferment or self-elevation. Some may not feel 'complete' Christians unless they have hands laid on them. Those who think they will not make the same mistakes as those already ordained are deluding themselves; sooner or later, they will end up being 'devoured by the system'. Some believe ordination will bring them closer to 'the people', but Ross claims their new role will in fact cut them off from parishioners, as 'people will either abuse them or tell them only what they want to hear'. She offers other reasons why women and men want to be ordained, such as desiring to be 'special', with more cynical candidates duped into thinking that the priesthood is an undemanding career. Some reckon they can play the role and survive, but in this scenario Ross thinks they are just bad actors.

'Ordained people seem to withdraw from their own humanity by artifice, by fulfilling a set of clerical stereotypes and pro-jections inflicted on them by institution and laity alike,' Ross postulates. 'The problem is that if someone withdraws from their humanity in the service of the church they're saying that Christianity is not a religion of the incarnation – and something not of this world. They are saying that to relate to God you have to reject what God has created and called good – and through which God engages in the world. This observation is not popular among the clergy but it is an honest view. Something dreadful seems to happen to people when they are ordained.'

Ross believes no woman or man has a right to ordination. She explains that ordination does not bestow the humility of Christ which, she says, is priesthood. As a contemplative, she has always believed her vocation was to Christ's priesthood in her being and not to function as part of a power structure.

There may be those who would want to challenge Maggie Ross on these points, but ordained ministry is not always what it appears to be from the outside. It has its own culture and not everyone drawn to it (for whatever reason) fits in. It is easy to idealise 'the church', only to find that the people we put on a pedestal have feet of clay after all. A collar around the neck is not the spiritual equivalent of a halo around the head, and you won't need to dig too deeply to find someone who has been wounded by 'the church'. It is important, though, to clarify what we mean by 'the church'. Thomas Merton once reassured an angry friend that the true church was not the institution, hierarchy or formal organisation 'which so hurt you as a child and which is now the target of your rage' but a living community of love: 'Now you take what you want and what you need and what is good from that other so-called "Church" ... and then you go on and live your life in joy.'[16]

Some clergy seem less inhibited these days from acknowledging publicly the failings of the church. In one parish magazine, the priest was commenting on surveys which had shown that people who had stopped practising their faith found it increasingly difficult to return to church, especially if they had been away for a long time. He then admitted that in the past

the Church has, in some instances, been guilty of being too dictatorial and even heavy handed in its dealings with people. The actions of some in the Church might even have caused their fellow Christians to suffer serious injustices and it would be insincere not to acknowledge that this has been the case. The Church is humbler today than in the past and does apologise for those failings. As a parish, we recognise that the Church has to accept each individual as they are and more importantly accept their anger and their hurts. We would particularly want to extend a welcome to those individuals, and where possible, we would want to help heal those hurts.[17]

Liberating Priesthood

The Irish philosopher and poet John O'Donohue, who eventually left the Catholic priesthood to write and lecture, claims ordination makes sense only against a wider and deeper backdrop of human priestliness: the place where the infinite and the eternal are glimpsed and felt. In this primal understanding, every person is a sacrament, an active and visible sign of invisible grace. We might also say 'a presence of God'.

O'Donohue maintains that each of us is called to be priest, ministering at 'this vital threshold where the eternal transfigures time and where the divine heals the human'.[18] The priest is not the isolated figure exclusively chosen with a gift others do not have, but the presence in whom the implicit priesthood of the human family is called to become explicit and active. More often than not, in the course of their ministry, ordained priests encounter people infinitely more spiritual than them, people who have travelled further on the path of mystical transfiguration.

There is an innocence and idealism about young seminarians longing to serve the broken thresholds of suffering and poverty, but the system ends up turning out clerics instead, he says. For O'Donohue, a real priest is someone who lives from the inside out, whereas a cleric is someone who tries to be a priest from the outside in, adopting the clothes, attitudes and behaviour of the system. The clerical mantle is paraded with little question or critique. Conversations are rarely real or penetrating.

O'Donohue hopes the destruction of clericalism (which cannot be divorced from discussions about abuse scandals) will eventually lead to the liberation of priesthood. In its true sense, priesthood is one of the most beautiful and creative forms of life. A real priest is one called to minister at the thresholds of greatest possibility and vulnerability, a committed witness to the invisible world which secretly embraces, sustains and gathers all the outer events of experience and life. But such a person can only give witness if already attuned to the thresholds in his own heart and experience. Rather than delivering 'a ready-made deposit of language and conviction' in a clericalist mode, the true priest is one who has 'the courage to attend with graciousness and expectation at the thresholds where experience yields to the crumbs of grace. There he gathers the bread of life.'[19]

In this sense, I suppose I now feel more like this kind of priest because, freed from the shackles of an institution, I am able to minister freely again at the thresholds of many different worlds. But this is part of one person's unique journey and there are, of course, various ways of understanding what 'a true priest' is.

If the 'vital tension' of the threshold is evaded or compromised, O'Donohue warns, the dualities will seize up. Then priesthood will no longer be a conversation with the eternal but will collapse into clerical functionalism. Minding these 'vulnerable frontiers of the Spirit' demands immense tenderness and compassion. If a priest endeavours to inhabit 'the integrity of his own inner conversation', he will not be driven defensively to control his people through judgement, blame or power. In work and presence, the priest remains 'a true doctor of the soul'.[20] In liturgy, word and ministry, the priest is the one who opens up presence for people and exercises a ministry of recognition. In accompanying people on their spiritual journeys and through their human trials, the priest seeks to make the divine presence explicit in a variety of situations, embracing imagination and experience.

In terms of identity, Jesus is in himself the threshold where divinity and humanity interflow. His person is the creative tension and balance of both dimensions – full humanity and full divinity. Jesus is also a threshold within Judaism itself, through whom an ancient tradition crosses a frontier into a new world. This is 'a deep aspect of his loneliness'. There is no mirror in his own tradition for him to image what is awakening in him. Time and again, Jesus has been functionalised as a safe and respectable presence. 'We have chosen to forget the immensity and danger of what was coming alive in him,' O'Donohue insists:

> As a priest Jesus inevitably sought out the vital thresholds where the real energy of his culture was. He trusted completely the unique shape and direction of his individuality. The task of his destiny was far beyond narcissism and egoism. The ultimate logic of his individuation was death. His faithfulness and attention to his inner conversation attuned him powerfully to the thresholds of possibility in his culture. Priesthood has much to learn from the courage, dignity and danger of his priesthood.[21]

Without doubt, John O'Donohue offers us a contemplative, if controversial, vision of ministry. Sister Jean-Marie Howe has also written engagingly on the notion of what she terms 'spiritual priesthood'.[22] We are on a journey from image to likeness which transforms our being and can ultimately create in us a state of spiritual being that derives from a deep participation in the life of Christ. At this profoundest level of spiritual life, our being, united to Christ's, becomes a channel of grace which saves and heals the world. This is sanctity, which is not to do with perfecting the self or attaining to virtue, but is of another order, a process of divinisation. It is no longer 'I', but Christ who lives in me, and this life of Christ in me transforms the world. This is how we become the presence of God for others.

The road leading to this order is, as we have seen, the way of kenosis, the death which must precede new life or rebirth. Transformation is dependent on the emptying of the self, engaging the whole being. This is inherent in the contemplative life. Immersion into the mystery does both the emptying and the filling. The mystery must work on us.

Howe writes that in order to receive the free gift of Christ's fullness, we need the desire and the disposition of emptiness which is also a prayer. She gives as an illustration the image of an incenser (or thurible). Its emptiness is filled with incense which pours forth in clouds of smoke into the surrounding atmosphere. Likewise, the incense of 'spiritual being' flows out of a monk's emptiness into the world as both adoration and intercession. It is this image which symbolises what Howe defines as a 'spiritual priesthood'. Our capacity for God, self-emptying, rebirth, and spiritual being all lead, not only to a personal transformation in Christ, but also to a universal cosmic transformation of the entire Body of Christ. As we are part of the mystical Body of Christ, our journey is one with all humanity (past, present and future).

It was Graham Greene's *The Power and the Glory* that helped Howe crystallise her thinking on spiritual priesthood. The novel takes place in Mexico during an anti-clerical purge. The last remaining priest is being hunted. He has lost everything: the honour and dignity of his role in society, material security and the human respect of the remaining faithful. His failings have become well known to all and yet it is precisely against this background of human frailty that his fidelity and passion for the exercise of his priestly functions (notably the Mass and confession) comes through even more forcefully. At the height of the persecution and the banning of the eucharistic celebration, wine is not only difficult to secure but also dangerous. At one point, Greene states that what the priest wants there and then is wine: 'Without it he was useless.' In a later scene, the chief of police is drinking the very wine that the priest, at the risk of his life, has finally managed to unearth so he can say Mass. The cleric cries: 'I see … all the hope of the world draining away.'

In the novel, the focus is on sacramental wine and sacramental priesthood. But the story helped Howe discern another wine and another priesthood: the wine of spiritual being and spiritual priesthood which has 'the power and the glory' to save and heal the world. Howe writes:

I believe that our capacity for God is our power and glory, for it can grow and be transformed into the wine of spiritual being. In order for this to happen, we must pass through a winepress, the winepress of kenosis. We must become new wineskins. For, as without wine, the priest in the story was useless; without the development of our capacity for God, we too are useless. Without the development of this capacity for God, I too see the hope of the world draining away.[23]

Spiritual priesthood means to be an intermediary between God and man, not by sign but in reality. The priest is in a state of mediation between God and humanity by means of a sacrament, a sign. Yet, Howe posits, we too can help the world through a spiritual meditation, a spiritual priesthood that draws its efficacy from the reality of our spiritual being in all its fullness. Spiritual priesthood is dependent on the awakening, development and transformation of our capacity for God, the foundation of our spiritual being.

'The capacity for God is the power and glory of the monk, of every Christian, of every human being,' she says. 'It is the image of God in the depths of the heart, containing the fundamental dynamism of our being: the image seeking its likeness.'[24] Within the heart lies the insatiable longing for our homeland and this indicates our radical need for God. It is from here that the movement of return to God occurs. This fullness of spiritual being can be transformed further by the grace of God becoming a river of wine that is fire burning in complete emptiness to heal and save the world. Such a person becomes a Spirit-bearer but, she explains, without lustre, because it takes place at a depth which escapes the senses: 'In the lives of certain people we occasionally glimpse something of this deep truth of spiritual life. They then become for us beacons of hope, lighting up the obscurity of our journey homeward.'[25]

Holy Love

Although my sojourn into ordained life took me into the desert, it was not altogether a wilderness experience. My year in the seminary gave me insights into what a flourishing community of faith could be like. I even learned to play croquet, although I soon discovered that hitting balls through hoops with wooden mallets was far more competitive than contemplative. The intensity of praying, worshipping, eating, studying and relaxing together beside a log fire (sometimes into the early hours) forged spiritual bonds I could not have imagined. We cared about each other and there was a certain 'holy love' about some of the friendships that developed.

One of the most memorable weekends was the college pilgrimage to Walsingham. It inspired a short meditation on formation which I gave after Morning Prayer back at the college:

> In our journey towards priesthood, so much seems to have been stripped away as we re-orientate ourselves for an unknown future. But as the German mystic Meister Eckhart put it: 'We grow by subtraction.' The whole process of training is a supremely Lenten experience as we discover that we are both broken and blessed, vulnerable but held.
>
> Formation is about learning to grow together and being open to unexpected discoveries. Last weekend, during the college pilgrimage to Walsingham, five of us made an impromptu visit to Holkham Beach on the north Norfolk coast, home to the pink-footed goose and a maze of creeks and salt flats, sandpits and pinewoods.
>
> After a long trek to the windswept tideline, we entered a liberating space of extraordinary beauty. The interplay of light beguiled, as the dusk seemed to anoint us with wonder – the ochre glow of the setting sun, tinted whisps of cloud in a darkening sky, flocks of larks and finches on the horizon. Each seemed to play a part in orchestrating a mystical melody as we gave thanks to the divine artist for the joy and

vibrancy of creation – a canvas charged with the grandeur of God.

And here, at the blue-green water's edge, five people, from different parts of the globe, unknown to each other until quite recently, were now together on the same priestly journey, experiencing the eternal now. It was, just for a minute or two, a moment out of time, clothing us in grace and binding us ever more closely into one body in Jesus Christ.

Lent is a time to renew our spirit of gratefulness for this unity. The more thankfully we receive what is given to us in formation, the more deeply we enter into the mystery of our calling – and the wild beauty that lies at its heart.

I was hugely impressed by seminarians and staff alike. When we eventually parted, there were emotional farewells as we knew we would never all be together under the same roof again. Most people, I think, were relieved to climb the wall. But although there had been an initial reluctance on my part to engage with an institutional lifestyle (as I was anxious about the clerical side of the calling), in the end I just could not bring myself to part from it. I even stayed on for a further ten days after the leavers' service. By then the place was like an abandoned ship and I felt like a stowaway. When my time really was up, I drove solemnly for about an hour until I reached the Hampshire town of Whitchurch, found a coffee house and diluted my large cup of Americano with a tearful acceptance that this way of life was over. I had become extremely close to a lot of people. It had been like a gap year in middle age that I didn't want to end.

I asked four of my closest pals from those days to tell me how they felt they became the presence of God to others in their respective ministries as full-time priests. I began with Lee Taylor, who spent a decade as a verger at Southwark Cathedral before training for the priesthood. A liturgist and organist, he is now a priest in London where he continues to be in a civil partnership.

Worship and mission are often seen as distinct activities in the church, he points out, and liturgy has certainly had a marginal place in discussions on mission in theological colleges. 'For me, worship feeds and nourishes our missionary activity,' he says. 'It shapes and forms us to be missionary people. The people of God are called to worship and be a transforming presence in the world by participating in God's mission. Priesthood should be about engaging and involving people in the great drama of worship, drawing them into a deep and regular encounter with God through scripture, the sacraments, symbols and action. Worship, of course, looks forward to the completion of God's mission – the final consummation – when we will experience the splendour of God's presence in all its fullness.'

Lee's pastoral work flows out of the liturgical life of the church. He sees himself becoming the presence of God to many different groups of people: the 'faithful and active few' in the parish whom he meets daily through regular services and outreach activities; the sick, elderly and housebound who receive holy communion at home, yet once faithfully attended the church; the children at the local primary school who watch enthralled as Lee stands in front of them making God relevant to their everyday lives; those on the fringes, such as baptism couples and the bereaved, and local people, who might not come to church, but whom Lee passes in the street at the same time and place every day as he goes about his ministry. This tends to be at the bus stop as he is walking to Morning Prayer.

'I believe that, by engaging in chit-chat, offering a kind smile, being a reassuring person and entering the door of someone's home, God's love in our lives is made powerfully present,' he explains. 'Talking to people about the challenges and common experiences of everyday life shows them that God is interested in all of us and actually shares our emotions and concerns. Our story has a place in the great story of God's purposes and journeys with us along the road of life. For those who are going through a difficult time, especially during a bereavement, simply being alongside them shows them that God weeps with them too and shares their grief. Our presence, as priests, represents the care and compassion of our divine Shepherd.'

Shortly after he was ordained deacon in Essex, Lee conducted a funeral for a woman who had died of cancer. Although the family were not worshippers, they requested that the funeral take place in the church. 'I visited the husband and members of the family a couple of times before the service and we corresponded a lot by email and telephone about the particulars,' he says. 'They seemed grateful and touched by the way I took the time to be alongside them in their grief. They also said they were moved by the words spoken at the funeral and asked for a copy of the homily. They had apparently been comforted by what I had said.

'A month later, an event was being held at a local café to raise money for a cancer charity and I went along. It had actually been planned by one of the granddaughters. All the family were there and my presence seemed to be important to them. The widower said he would like to keep in touch and meet up sometimes. He explained that he had never been a religious man as such but felt that my "obviously firm faith" could possibly be helpful to him as he continued to grieve for his wife. I have continued to journey alongside this family, trying to show them that God's light is stronger than darkness and death. For me, love, community, relationships and being alongside draw others into the heart of God.'

Another seminary friend became a curate in the picturesque Suffolk town of Lavenham. Mark Woodrow formerly worked for a major insurance company with spells in India. For him, it was not an easy transition from seminary (where there was space set aside for prayer and contemplation) to parish (where he has been largely in thrall to the existing practices).

'This is something I have found to be personally dis-appointing,' Mark admits. 'Deacons are charged "to be faithful in prayer, expectant and watchful for the signs of God's presence, as he reveals his kingdom among us". The reality is that, in order to be "faithful in prayer", I find myself having to "fight" to find space among my responsibilities and expectations to be alone, to be still, to be open to God in prayer and, indeed, how I pray. There have even been times when I have found myself feeling guilty about taking time out to pray.

'I find that I can no longer achieve the stillness I need to pray deeper, especially if I am home, in my study, or even in one of our churches – there are simply too many other distractions, jobs which must be done or telephone calls to be returned. I now find that, in order to pray deeper, I need to escape the parish boundaries. I cherish more than ever the sanctuary of retreat houses and monasteries where I can be alone with God and, at the same time, share the company of others who are seeking a better understanding of God. And sitting alone on the coast, breathing in the sea air and allowing God to still my mind and speak directly to my heart have become places of intense calm and fruitful spiritual nourishment.'

Mark says his ministry to others is a 'ministry of presence', being available to all in a village who are 'looking for something'. He offers a reassurance that God cares unconditionally and understands their urge to pray, even when they are not sure who or what they are praying to. At the same time, one of the blessings of working in a tourist location is the number of visitors. Mark prays with them and they feel able to speak to him openly as a priest as they are detached from their home lives. They feel safe in being honest because they know they are unlikely to see him again. 'In a small way, I hope to be the loving, compassionate and understanding figure who, in their time of need, stands in the place of Christ but always pointing to the One who has called and sent me,' says Mark. 'But my desire to be available does come at a cost. I believe that through my ordination as both a deacon and as a priest I have been forever changed. I am here to work alongside the Holy Spirit and be Christ-like to all whom I meet. Like Christ, who is always there, my ministry is a 24/7 commitment. But it is a burden I willingly accept. This is why I need to be still with God so that I can share with him the sadness, disappointment and pain which I cannot fail to take on in the course of my work.'

For his first Christmas morning sermon on the English-Welsh borders, Chris Johnson took to heart the idea of Christ being the image of the invisible God and that we are all made in God's image. He then produced a small shaving mirror which he passed around the congregation so members could look into it and see themselves as reflecting God's image. One young man, who happened to be visiting the church that day, later said the service had enabled him to see himself 'in a whole new light, loved and accepted by God'. In due course, he even asked to be baptised. 'So while I may not have been the presence of God for him,' says Chris, 'I suppose that I enabled God's love and presence to be known that day. I find it humbling that God works through us, and sometimes visibly through those who do his work. The eucharist has always been a time when I've been acutely aware of this happening. Now that I am privileged to preside at the altar, I always try to bear this in mind as I share in tending the flock of the Good Shepherd.'

Chris, who is curate of a group of parishes in Herefordshire, is the only son of an Anglican priest. An organist, he read theology and music at Canterbury Christ Church University in Kent before following in his father's footsteps. 'The great joy of rural ministry is being able to get to know – or be known – by people more easily, I think, than in an urban context,' he told me. 'Sometimes this can simply be manifested by visiting an elderly person for a brief chat or a cup of tea, even on an infrequent basis. I've noticed that this can brighten someone's day quite noticeably. I would suggest that this brings the presence of God to people very effectively.'

Celebrating the eucharist and saying the Office, the official prayers of the church, also provide moments of collectedness and calm in the throes of a hectic week. It's not unusual for Chris to clock up 300 miles a month driving around his parishes. The punctuation of morning prayer, along with a midweek service of holy communion, helps him ground parish life in 'something deeper'. In the car between engagements, he sometimes offers 'arrow prayers', brief intercessions of perhaps only a sentence. These, he says, maintain the priestly imperative to remember people in prayer before God.

'A small group of us, lay and ordained, are committed to saying morning prayer every Monday morning in rotation around the seven churches in our group,' he points out. 'This means the life of the churches is rooted in prayer, especially those buildings that are not worshipped in every week.

'One of our churches is a beautiful building with Jacobean fittings – but without electricity. It's located at the end of a long, green lane about a quarter of a mile from the road. It is now inaccessible to elderly and infirmed parishioners. Much as they love it, they can't meet there any longer. So every month we have a short communion service in a parishioner's living room where it's warm and comfortable. This is another way of bringing the sacrament or presence of God to people in their homes.'

When Myles Owen is saying prayers at his church in the celebrity belt of North Cheshire, he knows he could well look up and find the paparazzi walking furtively down the aisle. His parish is home to multi-millionaire footballers, cricketers and soap stars, whose children sing in nativity plays and harvest festivals – and need baptising too. It's not uncommon for famous parents to start chatting to Myles at school events. It's clear from his uniform what his role is but he doesn't always know what *they* do. So he likes to ask them and sometimes receives the casual reply: 'I play for Manchester United.'

Myles is the son of a former soldier who became an electrician in the television industry and worked on *This is Your Life*. Much to the bewilderment and disappointment of his parents, who hoped he would join the armed forces, Myles began to explore a vocation to the priesthood and read Biblical Studies at Sheffield University.

These days Myles sets about his ministry on foot and pedal. After evensong on Sundays, he keeps his collar on and crosses the road to continue his mission – in a pub. Here he joins choristers for a pint or two, but often it takes time for him to move from the bar to the corner seats because drinkers want to talk to him.

One Sunday, with a glass in his hand, he was exchanging the usual pleasantries with a regular when he spotted an unfamiliar face on the same table. 'Looking at the stranger's demeanour, I was certain he had something weighing on his mind but I didn't let on what I was thinking,' says Myles. 'I introduced myself with a smile and expected the usual banter. But instead, the stranger opened up a greater conversation between us. We talked about all manner of things, including football, and I hoped I might have managed to show the human face of the church and the Christian life. That, I thought, was that.

'Then, a month later, I received a call from a woman and discovered she was the mother-in-law of my new-found friendly acquaintance. With great joy, this lady thanked me for talking to her son-in-law. For a moment I couldn't remember who she was talking about.

'I learned that the stranger I met in the pub was actually married to a churchgoing Christian woman (the daughter of the lady on the phone). There had been a long-running argument in the family about having the children baptised. For the mother it was crucially important, but the father despised the idea and had banished thought of it completely.

'The mother-in-law was thanking me because the morning after the father had met me in the pub, he had decided that baptising the children *was* probably the right thing to do after all. This, I was told, was a complete U-turn.

'I do not know anything about the father's relationship with God. I suspect he talked the talk of an atheist but walked the walk of an agnostic. In any case, he was hostile towards the church and, as far as I can recall, hostile to God. By meeting him on his own territory – the pub – and demonstrating to him that we clergy are human beings like him, I suspect that I helped dispel the myth that the people of God are first and foremost anything other than people. Indeed, a Christian is as much a part of God's creation as any other human being. I am actually uncomfortable with the idea that we become the presence of God, but see myself more as pointing to God, the work he is doing and the work we all share in.

'In all that I do, I am nothing more than an "unworthy Levite", a servant of the Lord. And yet, if I work with and for and in the name of the Lord, then surely I must from time to time leave an imprint that more closely resembles His hand than it does my own.'

Myles explained that, in the pub that night, without intending it, his conversation had changed not only a man for the better, but also his view of the clergy, of the church and of God. 'This was not my doing,' Myles insisted. 'I spoke to him about football and he asked me a few questions about my vocation. I raised a pint with him wearing a dog-collar but he would not have been aware that, at that time, my prayer life was in bits and my sense of calling riddled with doubts. So this was not me deliberately setting out to influence his position. I even struggled to re-member the conversation. It is not down to us whether our work bears fruit – it is not even our work that we do.'

6

The Blessing of Light

Glory be to God who has shown us the light!
Lead me from darkness to light,
Lead me from sadness to joy,
Lead me from death to immortality.
Glory be to God who has shown us the light![1]

I often start the day with this invocation of the light and sometimes use the prayer when visiting those burdened and imprisoned by darkness of one kind or another. The words came into their own one grim winter's day when a friend was taken ill after new medication treating him for depression clashed with the old. A GP had wrongly told him to stop taking some tablets that weren't working, instead of explaining that he should ease himself off them gradually. The result was catastrophic and frightening. On a rainy December evening, with Christmas carols in the air, I drove in slow rush-hour traffic to get him to a hospital. There we waited, filling out forms, flicking through outdated celebrity magazines and drinking hot chocolate from a machine in brown plastic cups. Bored and fatigued, we even started inventing quiz games on scraps of paper to keep us awake. It was ten to three in the morning before we saw a consultant. My friend had brought a packed case expecting to stay and, although this wasn't strictly necessary, it was agreed in the end that it would be for the best.

Before dawn, he was moved to a secure mental health unit which was not really appropriate but provided the only available bed and treatment facility. With all its locked doors and strict regulations, it was difficult not to imagine that he was staying at Her Majesty's pleasure. After saying our farewells, I heard the door click behind him and watched through a small glass panel as he walked disconsolately back to his room. There and then I gained a sense of what real sadness can mean.

It had been some months since I had decided to step aside from ordained ministry and, as I had been strongly encouraged by many friends not to lose the identity altogether, I decided to don the uniform again. Although I often felt self-conscious in a white collar because I felt it identified me with the institutional church, I discovered that, in the mental health unit, it was a passport to another country. The young patients on suicide watch were mainly Roman Catholic and immediately assumed I was a priest in their tradition. I explained my position and soon realised how ecumenical people really are. They still asked for blessings. These men had clearly suffered in many different ways but nonetheless radiated the light of Christ in their lives. Despite their anxieties, they opened their hearts about their beliefs, spoke with astonishing conviction about them and shored up my own faith in the process. What was so apparent was that these young patients wanted to talk about spirituality and their experiences of it.

I noticed that one young father had a rosary tattooed on his body. He explained how he had confronted drug dealers in his neighbourhood because they were enticing ten-year-olds. The dealers had then sought revenge on him and his family. This had triggered a serious depression. Yet, in this clinical setting, where everyone was being observed every few minutes, here was a person with an extraordinary faith in God and a compassion for others that uplifted the spirits. This same man had lost his mother to cancer and had then decided to raise thousands of pounds for a charity. His life had been marked by poverty and tragedy, but he knew how to point others towards the light. As the Christian psychiatrist and writer, Gerald May, puts it: 'There are a great many souls walking among us who could be psychiatrically labelled as neurotic or psychotic yet who manifest such deepness and clarity of faith that they could well be *our* spiritual guides.'[2]

Everyone has the power to bless (and everyone has the ability to curse). Each of us has a vocation to bring light to others yet, in the process, we are often the ones to receive the benediction. On a pilgrimage to the Holy Land, with friends from the seminary, I visited many famous landmarks. But it was not only the sunset from Mount Tabor, a eucharist beside the Sea of Galilee or a baptism in the River Jordan that remained with me when I got home – it was something much less spectacular but nonetheless powerful.

Surrounded by gardens of orange trees, Holy Family Hospital in Bethlehem, 800 metres from the birthplace of Jesus Christ, is a large white stone building in the Arabian style. The hospital is dedicated to providing care for women and infants, regardless of religion or nationality. Yet, as we learned, there was an occasion years ago when its neutrality was violated by the Israeli army. A tank pulled up outside the hospital gates and started shooting at the surrounding buildings. The machine gun fire hit windows in the entrance, central corridor and laundry room where people were working. Bullets ricocheted and hit an intensive therapy room for the newborn where premature babies were sleeping in incubators. Cribs close to the windows were strewn with shards of glass.

The hospital's slogan is 'The poorest deserve the best'. Mobile clinics go into the Judean Desert to serve people living in tents and shacks where there are no sanitary facilities, electricity or running water. We were allowed to look into an intensive care unit where tiny figures were struggling to survive. What struck me immediately was the profound silence of the room, broken only by the sound of electronic bleeps. I looked to my right and was drawn to the sight of a Palestinian woman simply sitting and waiting beside her sick child. It was an image of selfless love and mercy. The presence of God to her newborn, the young woman possessed a serenity and compassion that moved me to tears. An artist could have replicated the scene as a modern pietà. I have cast my mind back to that ward many times. Peering around the door and simply moving on like a tourist would have been to miss a holy engagement. As the baby hovered between life and death, here surely for the pilgrim was an experience of the eternal now.

As I have already mentioned, when we develop a contemplative heart through prayer, silence and adoration, we become attuned to creation in a new way. We notice people, situations and landscapes with a greater sensitivity and perceive within them the divine artist at work. Our hearts expand with compassion when we communicate the love of God to others with gentleness rather than zeal. Some people can wear themselves out as they visit others with a compulsion that may arise from a feeling of guilt or neediness. But when we truly become the presence of God, we are offering our lives as earthen vessels for the healing of others as well as ourselves.

A contemplative in the world, aware of her deepest self and of her deepest need, is called to be a light of compassion, especially in places where darkness overshadows hope. It is simple enough to write about; living it is much more testing.

Wayne Teasdale believes that one effective way of developing compassion is to *intend* it each day – to think of it and reflect on its nature as part of each one of us. It should arise spontaneously from our spiritual practice, he says. Love and compassion are always the goods of the spiritual journey, guided by divine wisdom:

> Compassion, love, mercy, and kindness are the attributes of our true and common nature when we become freed from social conditioning and the indifference that often accompanies

ignorance. The mystical life awakens knowledge of our genuine nature; it is a path to who we really are. The more we pursue it honestly, the more we become aware of our innate love and compassion.[3]

He sees monks or mystic contemplatives in the mainstream of society as agents of change or reform. They have a vision of a human world animated by the best qualities of which we are capable, a world where 'compassion is alive, where love takes precedence over indifference, kindness over neglect, and mercy over oppression'.[4]

The Trial of Dementia

I can see the words hanging in front of me and I can't reach them. And I don't know who I am and I don't know what I am going to lose next … This might be the last year I'll have myself … I am not suffering. I am struggling, struggling to be a part of things, to stay connected to who I once was … So live in the moment I tell myself. It's really all I can do: live in the moment.[5]

These are sound bites from the trailer for the movie, *Still Alice*. They are spoken by the actress, Julianne Moore, who won an Oscar for her portrayal of linguistics professor Dr Alice Howland, who was diagnosed with early-onset Alzheimer's Disease at the age of fifty. The film is based on the bestselling novel by Lisa Genova.[6] Both book and movie have put the illness in the international spotlight.

Fifty is young enough. But the mind can deteriorate much sooner. Alzheimer's can affect people in their thirties and forties, although 'early-onset' implies under the age of sixty-five.

Many of us are presented with new challenges as we care for those with various forms of dementia. In recent years I have visited a cousin, a journalist friend and a close spiritual companion who have all succumbed to dementia-related conditions. It can be nostalgic when I dare to reflect on the conversations that used to go on between us, but those memories have stimulated our chats over mugs of coffee. It strikes me that becoming the presence of God in these situations is a delicate ministry.

Although many patients seem to be in their own undefined world, they are not beyond the reach of pastoral care. To learn more about the spiritual needs of patients, I turned to a daughter who nursed her mother through Alzheimer's Disease. Lesley Bilinda was, in fact, a friend in the seminary and is now a priest in London. 'As Mum's confidence rapidly diminished, she stopped attending the large morning service at her church, preferring the smaller, more intimate, gathering in the evening,' she told me. 'Initially folk were good about picking her up from home when she stopped driving and about chatting to her after the service. But sometimes, when I attended church with her latterly, I noticed people didn't make much effort to speak with her. After she went into a home and then into hospital, I was very disappointed that she received so few visitors from church, and hardly ever had a visit from the minister although she had been an active member and elder for many years. I think people didn't know how to respond to her disconnected conversation – and I think she knew she wasn't making sense and that embarrassed her a lot.

'I don't remember any staff – either in the home or in the hospital – ever having a conversation with any of the family about Mum's spiritual needs. Whenever I left her, I would leave running a CD of her favourite hymns, or Classic FM. Yet most times, when I came back the next day, I'd find the radio on and tuned elsewhere – at best Radio 2, but usually some pop station which she would never, ever, have listened to. I don't think that we did enough to help the staff understand the importance of Mum's faith. She'd always had a quiet faith and was quite private. She wasn't someone to shout about it, even when she was well. But I don't recall there being any interest whatsoever in her spiritual needs from any of the staff. Generally they were good about chatting to Mum and ensuring all her physical needs were met. Most treated her gently and with respect, and she generally responded to that. But one of the senior staff was very brusque with her and that brought out the worst in Mum. This particular nurse would march up to her and force her out of her chair without explaining beforehand what was happening – and then get angry with Mum when Mum fought back, punched, scratched or kicked. It made me realise how much Mum was picking up, even though she wasn't able to express herself much at all. And it made me realise what a frightening and lonely place she must have been in. Had there been a chaplain specialising in spiritual care of the mentally ill, that would have helped enormously in supporting us all as we tried to do our best for Mum.'

Lesley's experience points up the fact that church congregations themselves need to be educated in understanding older people, especially those with dementia or Alzheimer's Disease. They should be guided to continue conversations with members who become mentally ill and be encouraged to visit them when they are no longer able to attend services. This seems vital in establishing and maintaining a patient's connections with the recent past. Furthermore, care homes and hospitals should be open to receiving some training from church leaders in understanding the nature of holistic care – that all people are body, mind and spirit, and therefore meeting the spiritual needs is as important as the other two. Clearly, nursing staff may not be qualified to offer this, but a pastoral team from the church, or a minister, could shoulder responsibility for ensuring that such needs are recognised, even if the specialist nurturing remains in the domain of the local church community.

The Suscipe, by Ignatius of Loyola, is often prayed collectively by religious orders:

Take, Lord, and receive all my liberty,
my memory, my understanding
and my entire will,
All I have and call my own.

You have given all to me.
To you, Lord, I return it.

Everything is yours; do with it what you will.
Give me only your love and your grace.
That is enough for me.

But Dorothy Lynch, a member of the Sisters of St Joseph in Chicago (who took part in a groundbreaking study into the condition) felt unable to say the words 'my memory' because she was conscious she no longer had one. Her honesty was reflected in a BBC programme, *The Nuns' Story*, which explored the relationship between the order and the Rush Alzheimer's Disease centre in Chicago.[7] The fact that a group of women, living together in one place and at varying stages of dementia, could be evaluated over twelve years garnered new insights into the illness. The programme followed the nuns as they participated in medical tests. One nun was asked to name as many animals as she could but could only proffer 'cat'. She struggled to recall others but in the end told her supervisor: 'Something's been turned off in my head today.'

What emerged strongly was the nuns' dignity, serenity and acceptance of their condition, and that how we end our lives has as much value as how we have lived them. The centre's director, Dr David Bennett, spoke about how the loss of cognitive ability was 'dreadfully costly' and how it was important to lay down new memories for patients. He made a helpful analogy between the condition and a photograph album: 'Imagine you have a photo album that represents your life and every hour of every day you take a snapshot that summarises the last hour of your life. At the beginning of Alzheimer's Disease, you stop putting in new pictures so when you look in your album, there are no pictures from this morning, yesterday or last week. You have pictures from several years ago so you can talk about things that happened then but you cannot talk about things that happened in your recent past. Alzheimer's Disease is like ripping pages out of the book, going backwards in time.'

An ordained Methodist minister, who pioneered ministry to people with Alzheimer's Disease, thinks the crucial question for caregivers and pastors is how they can nurture a sense of spiritual well-being in a person with a diminishing ability to think, reason and remember. While it seems unlikely (within current understanding of the disease) that it would be possible to advance spiritual growth, it is never possible from a Christian viewpoint to discount the work of God's spirit in anyone's life. What we can try to make available is what has always been present and part of a person's spirituality.

As a teacher of early reading, Shamy had seen the developmental blocks of learning being put into place and being built up in a child. It was a progressive experience. As each new skill was mastered, another block was in position. But this was only possible after existing skills could be recognised and consolidated. Working later among older people with failing mental powers, she observed the reverse process: the developmental blocks were slowly being dismantled. But the question as to which abilities remained still seemed pertinent. Care workers, including ministers, should be encouraged to open up opportunities of making the most of the remaining skills which, Shamy believes, are lost too swiftly because the primary focus in some nursing homes is custodial rather than rehabilitative. Staff are not trained to recognise and nurture individual aptitudes, especially at weekends when employees change. Fortunately this was certainly not my experience of visiting my cousin at any time. There was great sensitivity among the staff to spiritual presence. On one occasion when I turned up in casual dress, an assistant asked why I wasn't wearing my clerical collar, even though I was going to spend time with a member of my own family who remembered me as a cousin and a journalist rather than as a deacon. My cousin did not know whether I was a church representative or not – in conversation he often mentioned my newspaper days – but he seemed always grateful for words of spiritual comfort.

Nevertheless, Shamy criticises clergy who refuse to wear a collar when visiting elderly confused people when they know that a simple change in clothing could provide a strong clue for memory-impaired people. 'These ministers are not willing to accept that small responsibility towards building a relationship,' she writes. 'They distance themselves and resist anything which may bring the cognitively impaired person closer.'[8]

Shamy believes all staff in the care home, and any visitor, should have the opportunity to nurture spiritual well-being for those unable to do it for themselves. Whenever someone grasps the opportunity to share community, to encourage relatedness, to reclaim, if even for a moment, a shade of identity, or to share a simple task of creativity, that person is helping to nurture the spirit, and heal and strengthen the soul. She identifies four useful tools for those who have a ministry among people with a primary dementia illness:

The first concerns principles of communication which is not restricted to the oral word (as any monk vowed to silence would confirm, she notes). Most people have choices in communication. The person with Alzheimer's Disease and related conditions is largely dependent on the efforts of others to make and maintain a relationship through less obvious forms of communication. It is important for ministers to learn to interpret body language and be aware of their own. Touch is important. Holding both hands focuses the person's attention. A smile is the shortest distance between two people.

The second tool is about orientating the person to the present reality, one different from the minister's but valid for the patient. It is the minister's responsibility to find a way to reach or communicate with that person in his or her reality, not to insist that the patient rejoins the pastor's reality. 'Hello Michael. I am Joanna. I'm the minister who visits you every Friday. We are at Dunston House. You live here and I am visiting you, Michael.'

Affirmation and response to feelings comprise the third spiritual tool. The minister may hear only nonsense and factual inaccuracy, but she neither colludes nor denies that. She is paying attention at another level. Behind the confusion, what she is hearing in the patient's feelings is more likely to enable her to reach meaningfully into his reality. If she can discern that, she can affirm feelings in that reality, being alongside him as a sympathetic friend and therefore in relationship as two human beings.

Memory-cueing constitutes the fourth tool. People with Alzheimer's Disease lose their recent memory first. Some of the remote memory remains, even in the most advanced stages of the disease. Memories are sometimes re-cued through the senses of smell or hearing. So a favourite perfume or aftershave, or a one-time musical favourite, might trigger the memory. The remembering of an experience from the past can be accompanied by feelings once associated with it, along with sensual responses such as colours, smells, sounds, music, voices and textures.

When we become the presence of God to others through our care and concern, to some extent we enter into their world and bring God's mercy to it. But sitting with a person suffering from dementia takes particular compassion and patience. This is where we are really being a light in the fog of memory. A tiring conversation may be interrupted by a man in the corner screaming incessantly, or a woman repeatedly coming up to join in. The friend you are speaking to may not want the other person to change the dynamic so, unless you go to your friend's room, it may be difficult to sustain much in the way of engagement.

Being the proverbial light in the darkness always involves perseverance, but at the same time a peace which the world cannot give is never far away. Sometimes the person you are visiting will be open to a blessing and this can happen without anyone else noticing. It is almost as though a cloud descends on the two of you in the midst of all the noise and confusion. But this is where the divine presence lies.

7

Bearers

It was not the telephone call I was expecting. On the line was an elderly man I had met only once. He reminded me that some years before he had been in touch about a project and had lost his cool. Clearly distressed, he told me that he had always regretted what had said, even though I could hardly recall the episode. He said he had been unwell at the time and had not been himself. Now he was dying of cancer and wanted to put things right.

It was a very moving conversation as he apologised for his error of judgement and asked forgiveness. I told him that, of course, I forgave him, words he longed to hear. I said he should put the matter behind him and be at peace. His sense of relief at the end of the line was palpable. We had one further conversation before he died – with greater serenity, I hope, than he might otherwise have had. The matter had been troubling him for years, but only in weakness did he find the inner strength to speak to me again.

Realising we're responsible for a breakdown in human relationships can burden us to an extraordinary degree, as our minds get tossed around in a sea of regret and sometimes shame. We can't put the clock back, but we can seek reconciliation.

The man's expression of sorrow and plea for forgiveness before he died reminded me of the vision of one man: Brother Roger Schutz. He founded the ecumenical community of Taizé in France, close to the medieval abbey of Cluny. From the Burgundian hilltop, Brother Roger and his brothers opened up new roads to heal the divisions of Christianity. They believed that the undivided church was the secret bedrock beneath all the churches. Unity, therefore, had to be discovered rather than built. As part of his mission, Brother Roger empowered young people from around the world to become 'bearers of peace and reconciliation' in their own cities, towns and villages. This is the spirit we need to imbibe in order to become a divine presence for others.

Inspired by the writings of St Augustine of Hippo, Brother Roger said Christian witness was about making one's life a reflection of the gospel. Communion with the living God touched what was most unique and most intimate with the depths of our being. Only a life of communion with God could lead us to seek reconciliation and alleviate suffering. The church did not exist for itself but for the world, so that it could place within it a ferment of peace.

The Rule of Taizé, which the prior wrote for his brothers, could be adapted for ecumenical contemplatives in the world.[1] It focuses on a community 'seeking to build itself in Christ, and to give itself up to a common service of God'.[2] Carrying the burdens of others, and being signs of joy and love, are among its precepts. 'Open yourself to all that his human,' the Rule states. 'Love the dispossessed' and those who 'thirst after justice'.[3] The brothers are encouraged to love their neighbours regardless of their political or religious beliefs, and never resign themselves to the scandal of the separation of Christians. If mercy is lost, everything is lost, so reconciliation and forgiveness lie at the heart of their vocation. Or as Brother Roger puts it rather poetically: 'All who root their lives in forgiveness are able to pass through rock-hard situations like the water of a stream which, in early springtime, makes its way through the still-frozen ground.'[4]

The work of reconciliation, integral to becoming the presence of God, can take us to the margins, the edges of the deep, the liminal spaces. Borders are not the safest of places but, as I discovered on many visits to Northern Ireland, contemplatives with a mission refuse to be compromised by danger. This was especially true of Sister Anna Hoare. In her late seventies when we met in Belfast, she was a familiar sight scooting around the divided city on her moped. The street in which she lived was actually on one of the dividing lines between Protestants and Catholics in the city. 'As I'm in the middle, people from both sides aren't afraid to see me,' the Anglican nun would say.

Sister Anna had a close-up view of life in Northern Ireland during some of its bleakest times, but she always believed that 'we all share a common humanity that enables us to live and work together'. Here was someone who clearly loved others and said it with her life. She personified contemplation in action.

Despite the violence on the streets, there remained 'something of the game in it' in terms of how the two sides related, she told me. On one occasion, while she was out of the area tensions began to mount and by the time she returned a full-scale riot was underway. Sister Anna spotted three groups of soldiers – one on the front line, another in the middle and a third on the outside. 'I approached the group on the outside and asked if I could go through with my bike,' she recalled. 'A soldier laughed and said I couldn't possibly because there was glass everywhere. So, suggesting I leave my transport with him, I asked if I could get through myself. The soldier chuckled and said I could ask the officer in charge if he would let me through. So I went to him and he asked me to go to the front line to see if I could get the rioting to stop. So I went to the officer and asked if I could get them to stop a moment so I could get through. I had to. He agreed, so I turned to the rioters and said, "Hi, would you stop a moment? I have to come through. It's important." They said: "Come on!" The rioters suspended throwing their bricks and the army stopped shooting at them with their rubber bullets. Everybody stopped. And I walked right through the middle and, as I did so, I said I would be coming back again and hoped they would stop again when I returned. I went right through. That showed me that it wasn't one hundred per cent serious.

'Another time I was coming down a main road and there was a cordon of women right across, not letting anybody through. Just by providence I was going to see a Republican prisoner and they were Republican women. I was on my moped this time. I said to them that I had to get through as I was going to this prisoner who was waiting for me. They knew him and all about him, so they melted like butter. I rode right through the middle. I might have been going to visit a Loyalist prisoner. It was just lucky it was the right side.'

Sister Anna's tenacity on the streets was matched by her pioneering work in helping to create the first Protestant and Catholic integrated school, Lagan College. What she achieved might have been radical in intent, but it had far-reaching consequences that perhaps not even she had envisaged. In a region torn apart by sectarian hatred and violence, her work brought Protestants and Catholics closer together in their living and understanding. There are now over fifty integrated schools in Northern Ireland, with a total student body of over twelve thousand.

Anna Hoare, who was born in Bath during the First World War, clearly remembered how her vocation had begun 'very definitely, at a distinct moment in time' when she was five. Until then there had been no divine awareness on her part but then it became obvious. 'I remember sitting on my father's knee. He was talking to me about God. I immediately knew that God was God and that he claimed me totally,' she said. 'I would be totally poor. I wouldn't marry. I would exist just for him. A small child is rather like someone with a mental disability – they go straight for the bull's eye. They don't rationalise.

'It wasn't an emotional moment. It was a matter-of-fact thing. There I was. There was God. He was my God and I belonged to him. I didn't know what that meant – the clothing of it. When I was in my teens I was thinking of going to China or India, of being poor and of not marrying for the sake of gospel in a rather muscular way.'

After her schooling and then obtaining a degree, Anna moved to Oxford where she completed her M.A. in Theology. 'I had an experience at university which fell upon me completely out of the blue when I suddenly realised the existence of the religious life, just like I had realised the existence of God, which again I had never really ever looked at or taken in at all,' she continued.

'That bowled me over because I think it's absolutely fantastic that some people can simply be created for God, not to be useful or serve any purpose unless he wants to use them in some way or another. Out of his own sovereign will, he chooses them to be there for him and to write a blank cheque which is what we do when we are professed, simply giving ourselves to God. He then takes it seriously and anything can happen.'

During the Second World War and beyond, Sister Anna was based at Wistow Training Centre where, with Gunter Schweitzer, she provided ecumenical training to refugees from Nazi Germany, lecturing in Old Testament Studies and early Christianity. During that time, she lived as a recluse and in 1970 became a professed contemplative. 'The very next day after your profession you can be struck down with deadly cancer and the rest of your monastic life you can spend dying,' she said. 'Anything that happens to you after your profession is absolutely fine because the essence is that you have given yourself to God. He has taken you and is using you in any way he wants. Whatever way that is doesn't make the slightest difference actually.'

Sister Anna attempted to live in her order's community but still felt God beckoning her to become a monastic pilgrim without any props. It was a radical intuition and one, she felt, her sisters did not appreciate or understand. 'It took twelve years for it to be proved. I was in one community and transferred to another. This peculiar vocation was to wander around the world without money, anything, or any connection with anybody, even the community. It was about depending on Providence and being led by Providence wherever he wanted to lead me. It was to be a life of prayer without any worldly support except the Lord.'

Later she received permission to be actively engaged as a social worker, travelling to Yugoslavia, Turkey, Israel, France and Greece. Then, in 1972, Mother Teresa of Calcutta asked the community to merge with her own order in Northern Ireland to develop its peace-building work; but as the Sisters of the Love of God were enclosed contemplatives they could not accept the offer. Sister Anna, however, who was in the distinct position of standing both within the community but beyond its covenant, stepped into the breach and headed off to the province where her unique vocation flowered. She never allowed even a fellow contemplative to dissuade her from following a path she instinctively knew had been mapped out for her. It was another example of claiming one's uniqueness and not allowing a personal calling to be compromised by any institution, even one committed to the religious life.

Sister Anna confessed to having had great prejudices about religious contemplatives. Nuns gave her the creeps, although she wasn't sure why. She didn't like them at all, but 'that was a prejudice and God can cut through prejudice, like a knife through butter'. She went on: 'God comes straight to the core of you. It doesn't matter what your clothes are. We've got to be woken up to have a certain thirst for him and to have a desire for simplicity, what in the gospels Jesus calls poverty of spirit. It isn't very attractive because of culture. You see people living in sophisticated cultures among rich people with bars in their drawing rooms, wonderful clothes and terrific parties. They have every kind of wonder and beautiful thing. They have got a lot of protective clothing around them and that is partly the *me* of them. It's not just the naked person but the person with all these things they've built up to make them feel they *are* something.

'It's partly insecurity and fear and not being liberated really that makes people want lots of money, status or power, or to be part of a gang if you're an adolescent. I would love not to have any of that. I don't want money, power or to be part of a gang. I want the opposite but I think it's the Lord who plants that in your heart and invites you to pursue that particular path which is to be free, to be united with him and to get rid of props which only get in the way. Socrates said that a human being was the greatest if he needed the least possessions to make him feel secure and be himself: if he was able to be himself with nothing. All of that is a gift of God.

'The thirst comes from him: to be uncluttered. Anything that makes people look up to you as somebody terrific gets in the way – between you and other people, and between you and God. I would rather have absolutely nothing, so that nothing gets between a prisoner I go to see or a small child who is only just learning to speak. I would like to be on the same wavelength with everybody, finding unity with every human being and, above all, unity with God.'

With this in mind, under the umbrella of an organisation that she established – 'Children's Community Holidays' – she initiated joint vacations for children from both confessions. As a result of this scheme, up to a thousand schoolchildren every year spend their holidays in Northern Ireland. For many, it is the first contact they have had with youngsters from another confession. Following the success of this programme, she began another initiative, 'All Children Together', and from this Lagan College was born in 1981. Through theological guidance and the political support of the community, Sister Anna worked with schoolchildren, parents and teachers. The college's purpose is to break down barriers of 'us' and 'them' by fostering a climate between reconciliation and understanding. Students from both denominations study together and learn how to coexist peacefully with one another.

After its opening, Sister Anna began to fundraise to get two chaplains of each tradition. In 1995 she established a foundation to ensure the school would continue to run smoothly and funds would be available in a strong spiritual atmosphere. She lectured worldwide on the political situation and the peace movement in Northern Ireland. She said young people needed to have the opportunity to learn about one another and to be tolerant about other denominations and religions. She also played a central role in the women's peace movement.

In 2003, at the age of eighty-six, Sister Anna returned to live with her community in Oxford and was registered completely blind. Her sight was failing when we met all those years ago but she seemed to accept it willingly. 'The more unselfconscious you are, the better,' she told me over tea in her home on the peace line, in a conversation that has always stayed with me as one of the most memorable interviews of my career. 'I don't really know who I am or what I am in a way. I know where I am going and what I want. When St Paul says, "I judge not my own self", I quite agree with him. I certainly don't. I just know I need the mercy of God. But when I stand before the judgement seat of God, all I will know is that I need his mercy. I won't know anything else and He will know what I am.'

Laughingly, she added: 'I haven't got any self-knowledge actually. I do go to confession at times. It is an enormous source of liberation and joy. I see my shortcomings very clearly and can make a nice list of them. I can see the substance of myself and it's pretty poor stuff. I am always aware of my need for the grace of God and the need for forgiveness. I'm aware that I'm putrid at the centre, if you like, but I am not upset by this because I know there is the power of redemption. Jesus was a specialist for sinners, not a specialist for the righteous. He couldn't do much for them.

'I had a very good start, a very united home and very loving parents who were very different from each other. I have a very strong base psychologically and, from that, I can go out. I'm not hitched up psychologically – I don't think I am – but I wouldn't say I had an awful lot of self-knowledge. Maybe I would have more if I had suffered more myself. I suffer really a lot through other people and through things that happen to them. But I don't really suffer through what happens to me.

'God showed us that there's no suffering to be compared with what he went through because he went through, not only the physical horror of crucifixion, but as he believed himself to be the Messiah and to be the Son of God, he faced physical extinction. This was not only a terrific act of faith but a terrible dereliction. Then everybody turned away from him – even his own chosen. Except a tiny handful, including his mother, everybody fled, denounced and betrayed him. All his life's work had absolutely crumbled and, after the faith he had put in, his heavenly Father didn't seem to be very helpful to him. That was the absolute extreme of spiritual, psychological and physical suffering.

'Because Christ was sinless, I believe, he faced the whole impact of sin, of corporate sin, the sin of humanity, of creatures, of the whole creation. He faced it head on and I don't think anybody has ever had any experience in any way comparable to that. It was utter desolation. Therefore, in our most appalling situations, he is there and is never absent because he has been through that. It was an all-inclusive suffering. He therefore suffered all our sufferings, all our little tiny sufferings. All of sufferings are absolutely nothing compared with his.

'In Belfast I think I have learnt about the power of God at work in the world. And that nothing is outside him or outside

119

his stretch. His hand is over everything and everyone, changing all to good and transforming everything.'

Trusting in God

During my reporting days in Northern Ireland, I met many people whose courage in adversity not only made remarkable stories for broadcast, but also shone more light on what becoming the presence of God could mean in the most heart-rending situations. One of them was Noreen Hill, whose husband, Ronnie, was badly injured in the notorious Enniskillen bombing of November 1987. Mr Hill had been the head of Enniskillen High School as well as a Sunday school teacher and lay preacher in the Presbyterian Church. On Remembrance Day, he had taken a Bible class and then gone with the children to the town's cenotaph. As they were standing on one side of a wall, a bomb exploded on the other.

Known as the Poppy Day Massacre, the atrocity killed eleven people – ten civilians and a police officer. Sixty-three were injured. Condemned by both sides, it proved a turning point in the troubles. The IRA said it had made a mistake. The target had been British soldiers parading to the memorial. The bombing later facilitated the passing of the Extradition Act, which made it easier to move IRA suspects from the Republic to the United Kingdom.

Mr Hill was completely buried in the rubble. His injuries included fractures to the skull, shoulder, jaw, pelvis and nose. He needed thirty-seven stitches to his head and facial wounds. Two days later, he went into a coma, in which he would remain until his death thirteen years later. Of these years, he spent four-and-a-half in hospital before being cared for in a nursing home bought by his wife. Mrs Hill introduced me to her husband in his electronic chair and I put my hand on his. He had a tracheotomy in his throat and a food pump attached to his duodenum. 'Give a deep sigh,' she encouraged him. 'We know you are listening, even though you don't open your eyes.'

For me, situations like these were always more than a means-to-an-end encounter for an illustrative reporting package. They had at times a quality almost as sacramental as sitting in front of the Blessed Sacrament. In this case, there was no doubt in my mind that I was in the presence of holiness being breathed both consciously and unconsciously.

The building was a twenty-bedroomed residential home in Holywood, County Down where Mrs Hill employed a nurse and three care assistants. 'He can't move, smile or talk,' she told me. 'But he can hear, he can see something – we don't know what – and he can feel. When the nurses have finished working with him, the position they leave him in is the one they'll find him in unless his bed moves. Ronnie doesn't move at all, except his head. He yawns sometimes and he swallows. We talk to him and tell him things. Yesterday I met the Prime Minister John Major who asked how he was. I told him that. We read the Bible to him, play CDs and he listens to a lot of religious tapes, especially sermons because he was a lay preacher.'

At the time of the explosion, Noreen had been suffering from cancer and had just finished a course of chemotherapy. But for all that had happened to both of them, she had never held any negative feelings. 'I was very weak and I could not have carried the burden of hatred and bitterness. I was able to forgive the people who planted the bomb but I know they have to go to God to get complete forgiveness. That is left between them and God, not me. They were never caught so they are not in prison. If they were caught, I believe they should be tried and sentenced.

'I've had to rely on God an awful lot. When Ronnie and I got married, we went out to Africa as missionaries, so God was a very big part of our lives. He has always been there. But after the bomb and when I had the cancer, I had to rely a lot on God. He didn't allow me to lose my hair, which would have been a calamity for me. I could always talk to God and he would always lift me up. I had to get all my strength from him and he has given it to me. Now I can go out and speak at different women's organisations and show them that there's no fear in cancer. I've come through it. I've come through a bomb. I have a husband in a coma but, because I rely on God all the time, I can smile and carry on.'

Mr and Mrs Hill, who had four children and four grand-children, devoted their lives to Christian service. But they had their share of anguish and suffering as well. Mrs Hill told me she had never lost hope and left everything with God. 'I think the one thing I have learnt out of all this is that I hand all my burdens over to the Lord and leave them with him. And that forgiveness is still there. The Lord has never allowed it to go away. I'm thankful for that.'

Mr Hill died in 2000, and Mrs Hill eight years later. I have never forgotten the couple, for each revealed to me what becoming the presence of God could mean, both passively and actively. The mystery of love was embodied in that husband and wife, who had given their lives for others and then experienced intense personal suffering. Service is not about earthly rewards. Mrs Hill bore no malice and even prayed for those who had planted the bomb.

The Path of Reconciliation

'There is a photograph of Gerard – that was taken the April before he was shot, the year he did his A-levels,' said Mrs Maura Kiely as she invited me into the lounge of her home in Belfast. 'He was really an exceptional child and he would not allow us to use fly killer in the house. When he was doing biology for his A-levels, he refused to do the dissection part.'

Gerard cared for all forms of life and all kinds of people. A student at Queen's University, he was one of two youngsters shot dead by Loyalists, who fired bullets indiscriminately across a Catholic congregation in 1975 in retaliation for the killing of two soldiers the night before. He was leaving church at the time. The murderer was the same age as Gerard and supposedly received five pounds for the killing. He was never convicted and was still walking the streets twenty-three years on.

'Forgiveness is imperative in the Christian life,' she said. 'There can never be reconciliation without forgiveness. People seem to think that if we offer forgiveness, we are showing a weakness of character. I really believe, on the contrary, that weakness is displayed in the desire for revenge.'

Mrs Kiely told me her faith was stronger as a result of what she had been through.

'When Gerard was killed, all I could do was to think of 2,000 years ago when Jesus hung on the cross and he said, "Father forgive them. They know not what they do." I wondered and I doubted whether my strength would be strong enough to allow me to do what I knew God expected of me at that particular time. I am very happy and very grateful that I got the grace from God and all the people who were praying for me to accept the cross that God sent our family that night in February 1975. But I firmly believe that He waited and he measured it. And he gave it to us then and said, "Take this cross and follow me." That is what he asked us to do. I live by my faith so I do.'

I also recognised similar depths of holiness in a man called William Rutherford who had been consultant in charge of accident and emergency at the Royal Victoria Hospital in Belfast at the peak of the Troubles. Despite his challenging work, he was a true bearer of peace. He had worked for twenty years as a medical missionary in India, arriving in Gujarat in 1947 just before Indian independence and witnessing the chaos and slaughter as Hindus and Muslims fled from Pakistan. Returning to Belfast, his experience proved invaluable.

'I think the most harrowing thing that I had to do was to tell wives, mothers, sons and daughters that their nearest and dearest was dead because of a bullet or because of a bomb,' he told me. 'At that moment, all those labels about unionist or nationalist, Protestant or Catholic disappear and people become just people.'

He recalled a woman knocked down by a military vehicle that had gone out of control after being shot at. Someone brought to the hospital what looked like a sleeping baby but was, in fact, her two-year-old child that had died. He also remembered a policeman whose girlfriend had been in for an X-ray. He had driven his car close to the hospital so that she could get in easily and he could drive away. But somebody suddenly spotted him and shot at the door. A minute later he was in the medical unit, but was already dead.

Mr Rutherford also cast his mind back to a day when inmates at the Maze prison had set their block on fire. They were left overnight in the burnt-out building because the perimeter was secure. In the morning, they were sprayed with CS gas before being shot with rubber bullets. Many were injured. They were all taken into accident and emergency. Then, all their relatives turned up, followed by vast numbers of soldiers with rifles trying to make sure the prisoners would not escape with them. It was a highly charged situation. There were fears that shooting would break out in the hospital if the wrong move or wrong command were made. 'I once drove into a riot and I remember being very, very frightened,' he said. 'Another time I drove to work and there was a workers' strike going on. I had to go through a crowd which was in a very ugly mood. Again, I was frightened. I think I knew that it was our fault and not God's fault. I wasn't angry with God.'

The son of a Presbyterian minister, William Rutherford said his faith did grow through his years in Belfast. 'The Troubles made me live very close to Catholic people,' he explained. 'It has been an enormous enrichment to me. I was very much deeper and stronger in my faith at the end of it than I was at the beginning. My thinking happened when I was in the car on the way home or lying in bed at night. When breaking news to people, one didn't talk religion. But I think God was there all right. I think I knew he was there and often the people who were with me knew that he was there.

'It was a great experience working with the whole staff in the department. We were totally mixed up: Protestant and Catholic, nationalist and unionist. Yet I never remember a single moment where I felt political conflict or religious bigotry inside that staff. I think I learnt the very basic humanity of everybody. Somewhere inside my head was the voice of someone saying that, if they had only known him, they could never have shot him. I think that goes for virtually every person who has been shot. The tragedy is that we have lived so much of the last four hundred years isolated from each other and not knowing each other. The great privilege of working in a place like the hospital was that both sides were forced to meet and you were made to realise that everyone was a person.'

But on the day we met, William Rutherford was honest enough to admit that he did have a certain ruefulness.

'I don't think I communicated this message of everybody's humanity enough,' he confessed. 'I don't feel I tried sufficiently hard to convince my Presbyterian church that peacemaking and loving your enemy are essential parts of our walk with God. I deeply regret that. The churches have done a certain amount but they have not done enough. Many of those people would say perfect love casts out fear. They would think that they believed it. But I think maybe all of us had a lot of fear in us and really our fear drove us into our ghettos.

'I think the churches were too silent. In ordinary church people's hearts, political fear and religious faith were fighting each other, and political fear won. So people got bottled up inside their own churches instead of their faith being the great thing that gave them courage to cross all the barriers – to throw their arms round the community and the church on the other side of this barrier.'

William was an active member of The Corrymeela Community, a Christian organisation whose objective is reconciliation and peace-building through the healing of social, religious, and political divisions in Northern Ireland. William helped set up a retreat house. He became the presence of God for others in many different ways, and one of them was by caring for patients in a way that extended beyond the treatment of their injuries. One Friday afternoon, a distraught woman from outside Belfast arrived at the hospital trying to find out what had happened to her son. He was a policeman who had been shot dead in an ambush. Unable to secure information, she feared a cover-up. But as the inquest had not been held, no information was available. After checking that his department was quiet and adequately covered, William took the grieving mother to the library where her son had been shot. She also met the family who had been held hostage in their house at the time and visited the son's police station where he had worked. After driving slowly behind the funeral cortège – of an IRA man – William took the woman to the station to catch her train home. Perhaps without realising it, William had become the presence of God for this woman. He had time for the mother in her sorrow, and she was helped in her bereavement by being able to see for the first time where her son had lived and worked.

However, as William Rutherford came to acknowledge, being a bearer of peace and reconciliation has to go hand in hand with justice. This is not always easy because we prefer to keep quiet and not rock the boat. As I have discovered myself, speaking against the tide can make the waters turbulent, and the support you might expect from others is not always forthcoming, even in Christian institutions. You are thrust into isolation. No wonder the Old Testament prophets ended up in the mire. But if we are authentic in our desire to become the presence of God, there may be times when, as part of that calling, we are required to stand up for what we represent. There can be no true peace without justice.

8

Befrienders

The hospital room was clinical and technical. There were machines, masks and medical apparatus, encompassing the motionless body of someone who, since childhood, had shared with me the joy and laughter of living. After many years of struggling with a degenerative illness, my oldest friend's health had dramatically deteriorated. I had seen him the night before battling pneumonia and then had arrived at the ward the following day a matter of minutes after he had breathed his last, his caring father beside him. A nurse said I could go into the room but not for long. As I closed the door behind me, I looked at my one-time school chum and invoked the name of the Holy Trinity in a spontaneous gesture of blessing at the bedside. I felt compelled, in those precious few minutes, to commend my friend on his journey to eternity. It seemed the most natural thing to do. I knew that neither a priest nor an ordained minister would be passing and that my vocation was to become the presence of God in that situation. Shortly afterwards, the nurse returned and politely asked me to leave. But I was powerfully aware of how, in the midst of a world of medical efficiency and clinical procedure, a sacred space had been created – if only for a moment or two.

Some years later, on an seminary placement, I learnt more about befriending death at a hospice that had once been an Augustinian convent. The plethora of corridors, along with statues and grottoes in the grounds, testified to the building's monastic past and a prayerful air of stillness seemed still to pervade every floor. On the day I arrived, nurses were beginning to put up Christmas decorations around the corridors and my first thought was one of sadness that most of those being admitted or already in residence might not live until the feast day itself. At times I wondered if I would be too psychosomatic a person to work entirely in this world, but also questioned whether or not the vulnerability I felt throughout my stay was, in fact, the character of a calling to 'share the darkness' with those for whom life was ebbing away.

In the chaplaincy office was a poster of waves hitting against rocks with the sun setting in the background. The caption read: 'The last part of life may have an importance out of all proportion to its length.' It was a philosophy that took on a particular significance as I accompanied the priest on his rounds. Many of the patients had been told by a doctor: 'There is nothing more we can do for you.' But the priest insisted that his role as 'spiritual care lead' challenged that assumption. I gleaned a great deal from him about becoming the presence of God at the time of death.

His ministry was about standing alongside someone with their feelings of despair, abandonment and hopelessness. He would talk with them about how they were feeling and this gave them an opportunity to open up. He listened as they unburdened themselves of fear and anger. The patients would be encouraged to talk about who they really were, their spiritual selves, what made them tick and what made them unique. 'I might talk about where they got their inner strength from in the past,' the priest explained. 'This might have meant engaging with nature, relationships or religious practice. I then try to ascertain, in the midst of their feelings, whether there might be an opportunity of re-engaging with that and so helping them on a journey towards accepting their state and facing death in a less hopeless way. They may then move towards death in a more accepting and embracing manner.'

Humour was often the key to deepening any relationship, 'like a cork being released from the bottle'. In the priest's experience, people with life-limiting illnesses did not always welcome hushed voices, pious chatter or serious conversation all of the time. They might ponder on the mystery of suffering or death, which could lead them to a state of mind that acknowledged the 'ridiculousness' of their situation. It brought no logical answer or sense, of course, so this could sometimes result in humour. Some patients looked at their physical weakening and laughed at their pitiful inability to be able to do what they had previously done with ease. Humour combatted embarrassment, broke down barriers and, on occasions, enabled patients to gain a sense of near normality. Humour was a great leveller and could lead to buoyancy of mind. It eased relationships for the priest, who could respond by facilitating whatever practices the individual or the family wished to engage in order to help the dying person find peace and acceptance.

I was reminded that people from many religious traditions, or none, are cared for in hospices. A multifaith quiet room enabled patients, families and staff to enter an oasis of calm. Tapestries, interpreting the word 'sanctuary' and created by members of an interfaith embroidery group, added an artistic dimension. For example, one picture featured the Manjushri Buddhist Meditation Centre in Cumbria, a holy place of refuge and peace; another reflected on the twenty-third psalm and the inner peace which God provided, but also illustrated water lilies emerging from the famous lotus flower in Buddhism that rose from the mud like a spirit arching over 'the muddled mess of life'.

The priest told me that often silence was the most profound response he could offer, although he might pray before a patient died. He memorised certain prayers, such as Psalm 23, or words from John Henry Newman. He might also offer prayers of guidance, comfort, grace, letting go, peace, light, joy and hope, woven together to address the unique situation of the individual. Another prayer might seek permission for a patient to let go in order to be released.

Holy oil could be used in an act of anointing before someone died. This involved marking a cross in oil on the person's forehead, accompanied by prayer and a request for the healing of the soul. Some patients might receive holy communion, sometimes in the form of the tiniest fragment of a consecrated wafer. The priest might then also offer a prayer of commendation, asking that the soul of a person be taken into God's care. Or he might say a simple prayer after death, giving thanks for that person's life, asking strength for the family and praying that God would receive, or already had received, the soul in tranquillity and peace. He saw himself as being 'a midwife of souls' but the lead should always come from the patient. The priest explained: 'If death is, in reality, birth into new life, then the chaplain is the one who stands alongside members of the wider team in attending to the person in labour – comforting, encouraging and facilitating as new life emerges from the old. There is something quite amazing about seeing people who are making this journey through the valley of the shadow of death. After their journey through this life is ended, one feels a tremendous sense of joy and peace, mingled with a profound feeling of being deeply privileged at having shared their Good Friday and watched the sun rise on their Easter Day.'

Transfiguring Fear

It was not the first time I had been to a hospice; my journalistic work had taken me there too. I remember especially visiting St Christopher's Hospice in South East London, established by Dame Cicely Saunders, who helped give birth to the modern hospice movement and its philosophy of caring for the whole person – body, mind and spirit. That day something unforgettable happened. After climbing the stairs of a nursing block, I glanced through an open door where my eyes met those of a patient sitting on a bed. I could not tell whether the patient was female or male, for the person was wearing a white gown and did not have hair. We just looked, deeply and fleetingly, into the heart of the other. It was a moment out of time. Such a deep serenity emanated from the room that I felt almost transfigured by the encounter. In fact, I even began to wonder if I had just seen an angel. The suffering person is an icon of Christ, often bestowing hidden and abundant graces. Carers are often called angels – and so they are. But patients, too, are bearers of messages, just like angels.

In the Middle Ages, St Francis of Assisi believed death should be greeted as a sister while, in more contemporary times, John O'Donohue saw death as 'the unknown companion'.[1] It was a presence that walked the road with you and asked to be befriended, accompanying your every moment, shadowing your every thought and feeling: 'When you were born, it came out of the womb with you; with the excitement of your arrival, nobody noticed it. Though this presence surrounds you, you may still be blind to its companionship.'[2]

O'Donohue (who was himself to die unexpectedly in his fifties) believed we were wrong to assume death came only at the end of life. Physical death is only the completion of a process on which our secret companion has been working since our birth. Our life is the life of our body and soul, but the presence of our death enfolds both. Death can meet us in and through different guises when we are vulnerable, frail or hurting. In every person there is a wound of negativity, like a blister on that life. This negativity is the force and face of our own death, gnawing at our belonging in the world. It wants to make us strangers to our own lives and hold us outside in exile from our own love and warmth. But we can transfigure it by turning towards the light of our soul so it can become the greatest force for renewal, creativity and growth within us. O'Donohue writes:

> To continually transfigure the faces of your own death ensures that at the end of your life your physical death will be no stranger, robbing you against your will of the life that you have had; you will know its face intimately. Since you have overcome your fear, your death will be a meeting with a lifelong friend from the deepest side of your own nature.[3]

Death also manifests itself every day through fear which falsifies what is real in a person's life, destroying its happiness and tranquillity. Many people are terrified of letting go, employing control as a mechanism to order and structure their lives. But at times of pain and, particularly at the time of death, it may not be possible to maintain that hold. O'Donohue continues:

> The mystical life has always recognized that to come deeper into the divine presence within, you need to practise detachment. When you begin to let go, it is amazing how enriched your life becomes. False things, which you have desperately held on to, move away very quickly from you. Then what is real, what you love deeply, and what really belongs to you, comes deeper into you.[4]

One of the ways of transfiguring the power of death is to transfigure fear. When you know what is frightening you, you take back the power you had invested in fear, he says. This also separates our fear from the night of the unknown, out of which every fear lives. All fear is rooted in the fear of death. O'Donohue was once at the deathbed of a friend, a young mother of two children, and watched as the local priest helped her to die 'as a friend'. As it became apparent she would pass away that night, she became frightened. So the priest took her hand and prayed hard into his own heart. As he knew her life well, he began to unfold her memories and spoke of her goodness, beauty and kindness. She was a woman who had never harmed anyone. She always helped everyone. He recalled the key events in her life. There was no need for her to be afraid. She was going home and there would be a welcome for her. God, who had sent her here, would welcome her. God would embrace her and take her gently and lovingly home. Of this she could be completely assured.

Gradually, a remarkable calmness came over her as all of her pain was transfigured into a serenity. The priest then invited each member of the family to go into the room for five or ten minutes so she could say farewell to them. They were to go in, tell her how much they loved her and what she meant to them. They were not to cry or burden her. Each one consoled and blessed her, before the priest anointed her with holy oil. Smiling and at peace, she went happily and beautifully on the journey that she had to make alone.

For the first time in his life, O'Donohue found his own fear of death being transfigured. It showed him that if you live in kindness, do not add to people's burdens and try to serve love, when the time comes to make the journey yourself, you will receive serenity, peace and freedom. O'Donohue believes the person entering the voyage of death needs a good deal of shelter (in the form of prayers) during the weeks after crossing the threshold:

> Death is the great wound in the universe and the great wound in each life. Yet, ironically, this is the very wound that can lead to new spiritual growth. Thinking of your death can help you to radically alter your fixed and habitual perception. Instead of living merely according to the visible or possessible within the material realm of life, you begin to refine your sensibility and become aware of the treasures that are hidden in the invisible side of your life.[5]

If we are to be authentic presences of God in the world, our priority must be to protect, heal and strengthen, to 'fore-brighten the world' for others, as O'Donohue puts it, making them feel that they belong. When death knocks at the door, our vocation is to befriend it by opening a window for someone into eternal time. The more contemplatively we live, the more instinctive we will become in recognising when we are being called to be the presence of God at a dying person's bedside.

I remember one bright spring evening when I learned that a friend in her late nineties was close to death. I sensed immediately that I needed to head to the nursing home at once. When I got there, the room was peaceful, lit up and warmed by the rays of sun streaming through the window. My friend's breathing was shallow and there was little sign of life in the bed. I whispered my name and she indicated by her eyes that she knew who I was. Then she reached out for my hand and held on to it tightly. I began to say The Lord's Prayer and, to my astonishment, she joined in with as much conviction as she had always said it. An inner strength surfaced from the reciting of that prayer. During the night, she died peacefully. There was no question in my mind that I had been invited to become the presence of God to her as she made the journey from one world to another.

It brought back memories of the day I went to see a lady who had recently celebrated her hundredth birthday in a nursing home, with all its professional busyness and the relentless sound of patients calling for assistance. A former Sunday school teacher, she spent day after day lying in her bed with her own thoughts. As I sat beside the rail, holding her hand and saying The Lord's Prayer, I felt an extraordinary peace and realised that, far from ministering to her, she was in fact ministering to me. As I stayed alongside my friend, who did not have long to live, there was an emerging sense that she was actually blessing me through her dying. As this was happening, rays of sun began to bathe us in strong light. I spoke to her about the atmosphere of resurrection and, just for a second, she looked ahead and exclaimed: 'Wonderful.'

Another spiritual companion of deep faith, who lived in the same home as the centenarian, had to be fed intravenously. She showed extraordinary patience in the face of her diminishment. She longed for a sip of tea but was not permitted to drink any fluid, only to moisten her mouth with a sponge stick. It always reminded me of Christ being given hyssop on the Cross. On my last visit to her before she died, she lifted her hand slowly and waved to me as I was walking out the door. To me it was the bestowal of a blessing from a lifelong friend.

Becoming the presence of God is not a one-way process.

During my year in the seminary, a fellow student was a GP who had looked after dying patients for nearly twenty years. Now a priest in Leeds, Dr Sheena McMain befriends death as a pastor. But in the surgery she had also seen herself as 'an accompanier on the journey' helping people deal with difficult news and coming to terms with a shortening of life. The scope of her care embraced not only the patients themselves, but also 'as importantly' their 'significant others', especially in terms of preparing them for a good bereavement. Patients need a supportive 'holding space' because a terminal diagnosis can be difficult to receive. Bad news takes time to penetrate. A doctor who begins probing and exploring options too swiftly can exacerbate an already difficult situation. An 'accepting space' allows a person to express varying degrees of anger, upset, confusion or any emotional combination. This can, in turn, yield to a 'hopeful space' for what is left and what is going to be. This might involve a discussion about the patient's quality of life now, as well as the anticipation and fear of death. The 'hopeful space' becomes, therefore, a 'listening space' where day-to-day concerns and other anxieties can be aired. Sometimes the GP's surgery, says Sheena, is the only place where these feelings can be vented; so doctors need to deal with each case with a gentle, compassionate realism, 'sharing uncertainty, acknowledging that what we have is what we have'.

Befriending death is part of the process of acceptance and needs to happen to everybody. There comes a point at which people need to make their peace with death. It is about patients feeling safe, having enough control to feel it is *their* life and *their* death, and that they have the necessary knowledge to cope. Most of them eventually reach a stage of inevitability. They might suddenly announce to their doctor that they have chosen hymns for their funeral or been to the solicitor to make a will. Sheena saw her role then as one of communicating the reality of death as a journey into something, an ultimate being at peace, but also pointing out that life is to be lived before death occurs. Most people know they are ill 'in some deep place' but might not be ready for that negotiation about their condition. Those already convinced of a terminal diagnosis might still react with shock and horror when it is confirmed.

'My medical experience has given me an understanding of many various and unique ways people react in the face of death,' Sheena told me. 'You have to be led by the person in the kind of way and pace they need, with an awareness that you are very rarely the only person involved or the most important. But it can be a very creative time when, for the patient, there is a lot of peacemaking and reconciliation with both themselves and others. There is also something about right timing, a journey full of those *kairos* moments, opportune times for having those conversations.'

Following a road accident, Sheena found herself reflecting on a life-threatening condition and facing the possibility that she might die. The fact that, as a physician, she had often had to deal with issues surrounding other people's mortality did not ease the process. She said she felt 'vulnerable and creaturely', adding: 'There was this sense of being mortally ill and feeling that sense of fragility and creatureliness. I wonder if that is at the heart of the dying experience for people, a journey everybody has to make on their own. Perhaps there are rehearsals during life through mini-death experiences but I think facing your own death is one of those critical moments. Much depends on how you feel you have lived your life, and your need to make peace with the life you have lived or haven't lived, the person you are and aren't.'

My father was forty-nine when he died of a brain tumour one wintry December night. He had been seriously ill for just seven weeks. But during this time he was able to tell me that, through his suffering, he had been given insights into the nature of God through prayer and the ministry of friends. He said that, no matter what happened, he knew he was held safe. He managed to walk alone to the hospital chapel to receive holy communion a week or so before he died. In those bleak, distant days, when my father was so unwell and so young, it was impossible to accept the inevitable or shape any coherent narrative out of what was happening on so many different levels. I presume I quietly trusted in God's merciful care and drew some comfort from the way in which my father was mysteriously befriending his own death. Despite his physical demise, there was a discernible spiritual growth. I came to realise how, even in the darkest of times, life could be shot through with the transcendent. The signs of God's grace in the natural world kept me harmonised with something bigger than my own interior distress. The tints of fallen leaves, for example, took on greater meaning. I believe there was something healing and redemptive in that.

Many years later, I learned more about the need to befriend death from the popular spiritual writer Martin Israel, who struck me as being every inch a contemplative in the world. He was in the autumn of his life when we met at his home in London. Parkinson's Disease was already taking its toll, but he was to live for another twelve years. As a pathologist, priest, mystic and psychotherapist, the South African medic had particular insights into spiritual development and the human condition. He talked about death in a most natural manner.

'I know more and more that death is merely a state of transition,' he told me. 'The physical body is discarded as an old piece of clothing or a motorcar would be when they have had their day. But the essence of me goes on from glory to glory.' Although 'the soul' might be considered an old-fashioned concept, it was nonetheless a consoling term and constituted the true essence of a person: 'that which is really me responds in terms of thought, emotion and relationship to what I would call God, a word that cannot be easily defined and yet you know is closer to you than yourself.'

Dr Israel said he was not surprised that people feared death, especially when their lives had been particularly selfish. If your life has been unclean, you begin to realise the future ahead of you might not be as good as you had hoped. But if, on the other hand, your conscience is clear, life after death can, in fact, be something to look forward to. Confessed sins can be forgiven and God's nature is always to show mercy.

The author said that he viewed his own death 'with increasing composure' as he moved nearer to it. 'I believe that, when I die, I will be embraced by love and I will move onwards. It won't be a state of being in heaven and in eternal bliss. To me that would be boredom of the most awful type. There is so much more to learn. It's so exciting in a sort of way. I've got to make friends with a lot of people who were unpleasant to me and vice versa of course. I believe reconciliation happens after death. I don't think we can be properly reconciled in our present state. We are far too limited on the personal and bodily level. I think that we will be more conscious than ever of our surroundings but I don't believe that time and space will be as they are now. This is something that is very difficult to explain. If you have had mystical experiences, as I have had (and lots of people have had near-death experiences and things like that), you are in a different milieu as it were. This is what makes it very difficult to put into words that ordinary people can understand because they are so limited, as we have to be. Our limitation here is our way of growth, but in the other sphere the growth is on a different level – and yet we are more perfectly ourselves than ever we are here. What I will be there is pure essence, as it were, and therefore I will be closer to God than ever before. God is absolute essence, of course.'

Heaven, for Martin Israel, was a state of complete love: a knowledge of God and a knowledge of love. He believed that we would all be one. There would be no separation at all. We would be able to be completely open without needing to hide anything. There would be no shame. We grow on and have to attain to the measure of the fullness of the stature of Christ. It is what we are all moving towards. We have to change. We should always be hopeful. The life beyond death and time would be much more evident to many people than it is now. The true mystic knew that. All people would see would be what was real and what was unreal: that reality was related to love and service, while unreality was associated with acquisitiveness and trying to get above other people.

'We don't even have to cast out fear,' he told me. 'If we are with God, God casts out fear by the love that he gives us. But if I were to tell you to stop being frightened, it would be a waste of time. You couldn't do it. But if I say "enter into the love of God" you will automatically lose your fear.'

According to the Benedictine monk Brother David Steindl-Rast, heaven is not a place somewhere else but everything transfigured by God's presence. For many people, therefore, heaven starts here, while for others hell begins here. 'Life that is transfigured by love and compassion and wisdom is heaven,' he says. 'It's not complete heaven, but it's a beginning.'[6]

For Steindl-Rast, death is not a sleep where we wake up on some other side. He believes there is nothing to indicate that and he would not even desire it. This 'now', he says, is plenty for him. He does not need to wake up anywhere else because he has all this. He cannot lose it:

I have my best moments that happened thirty years ago. I have them as much as time permits, in the sense that time always gnaws on them and sort of clouds them, but I have them now. I possess them. I can remember them, and in this memory they *are*.

'All is always now,' as T.S. Eliot says in *The Four Quartets*. When I enter into this *now*, which happens when time is up, that's what I call death. Death is that in which afterward, there is nothing. As I understand it, it's the end point of time. Anything else seems to be a little soft pedalling and a little too tame. It *is* the end, so I better make good use of the time that I have.

Death is that after which there is nothing, because there's no time after it. I do believe in beyond life, however, but most people who say that they believe in afterlife mean the same thing as life now.[7]

We have, Steindl-Rast points out, already experienced heaven (ultimate belonging) and hell (alienation from everything). In our best moments or 'peak experiences', we have encountered heaven. This taste of heaven is a moment in and out of time. Therefore it is not really in time. In a peak experience, it may just be a split second and seem like a long time, or it may be an hour and seem like a split second. We are in the present at that moment. Most of the time, half of us are hanging onto the past, and the other half are stretching out to the future. There's nothing left for the present moment. But in our peak experiences, we are really there, and this is *now.* That is where we experience heaven, the monk explains. He goes on:

When my time is up, when I die, time is up. I do not believe that time goes on for me. That's not death. There may be all sorts of surprises in store for me, but then that wasn't what I call death. There may be some other life after this life, but there's not much evidence for that, either. That's sort of an interpretation of other things. The way I see it, when I die my time is up, and I don't have to worry anymore about anything after. That's a great relief to me. If I had to worry about things going on and on and on, that would not be particularly helpful to me, for my peace of mind. But I have a measured time, and then my time is up.[8]

As we help others befriend death, we are likely to be asked what our views are on 'the beyond', even by those who profess no faith at all. Although it is impossible to give definitive answers, people deserve something more illuminating than vague sketches of what we imagine eternity to be like. Of course, we cannot be certain, but avoiding the subject is not necessarily appropriate.

There is, however, a much more casual approach to death these days and, at receptions after the funeral, sometimes the only person not talked about is the deceased. But there are also occasions when the manner in which death is befriended by a family is sacred and moving. I noticed this especially when a priest friend invited me to join him at a Travellers' wake. As we drew up in the car, in an ordinary street of a rural village, we noticed flames from a brazier and a marquee in the garden. Friends and relatives had planned an all-night vigil outside the house. Inside, white sheets covered the walls of the front room where the sixty-year-old mother lay in an open coffin, a crucifix above her. Her sons and other family members (who had earlier dug the grave and would later fill it in) joined us while we said prayers on the eve of the woman's funeral. They said they would stay with her until morning. There was a holiness about the occasion and a gratitude that representatives of the church came along too. Although we were there for only a few minutes, this is how we became the presence of God for others at a difficult time in their lives.

Love and Tragedy

The issue of suicide can raise particular issues for all who offer love and comfort to others at times of bereavement. I remember meeting a priest whose brother had taken his own life because it had become unbearable. He had been a productive man who had married and had a good job. But then he lost his wife through a divorce and his employment as a result of a court case, swiftly followed by his status and then his faith. From there on, it had been a steep decline until his untimely death.

'My brother felt he couldn't continue,' the priest told me. 'Curiously, we talked about the prospect of suicide a great deal beforehand. As a priest, I tried to assure him that he was not going to be judged in any way whatsoever, that the God we both shared was a God who was a loving God. Although I preferred him to live than to die, I certainly wasn't prepared to rob him of his own autonomy.

'He had made previous attempts so I was rather expecting it. It wasn't a shock in the end. It's only since it happened that I have begun to realise that what, perhaps, was really lacking in his life were those basic building blocks of love which he might not have received at the most important points in his early life. I thought as a priest I was going to be helpful. I ended up moralising and offering what I thought was good advice instead of really listening to the story and finding sufficient time and effort to really listen.

'That moment, when one desperately cannot go on in life, is perhaps the moment when God is very, very close indeed. I believe that the lonely moment when my brother died was a moment when he was very close indeed to his Maker.'

The priest revealed that he had come close to suicide himself many years before. We all have our own dark and black fears, he said, and his had been loneliness. 'I had spent so many years away from home, working as a professional musician, so I knew that the hotel bedroom could become a very lonely place – so

144

much so that, on one particular occasion when I was on tour, I couldn't really bear to go on for another day. So I took some drugs. I was working in the theatre at the time and under some stress. I certainly made an attempt on my life, cutting my wrists and taking drugs. I was astonished to find that, remarkably, I had survived.'

One of the most moving funerals I have ever taken part in was for a forty-year-old father who committed suicide. It was especially poignant because no one turned up and the crematorium was empty, except for the chapel attendant, funeral director, priest and me, acting as deacon. The man had become alienated from his family and friends, who lived at the other end of the country. So the four of us formed an arc at the catafalque, commended him to God and befriended in death a tragic and lonely figure about whom we knew virtually nothing.

Then, about two months later, a popular friend and well-respected professional in the town took his own life. This time the funeral had been meticulously planned, with choral music and eulogy, and was attended by four hundred. But what remains more vividly in my mind is the evening before when I met his older brother off the train and drove him silently to the chapel of rest. We walked in slowly together, consoled by the icons around us. Then I stood back and watched achingly as he placed an orchid into his sibling's hand. It was a gesture of fraternal love that twinned beauty with sorrow.

A similar irony struck me a few years later when I was in the mountains of Donegal, unveiling a memorial to twelve crewmen who had died in one of the last plane crashes of the Second World War. My uncle had been one of them. In the early hours of 14 March 1945, their Shorts Sunderland flying boat had taken off from RAF Castle Archdale on the eastern shore of Lower Lough Erne in County Fermanagh, Northern Ireland. They were on a U-boat mission to the Atlantic when, inexplicably, the plane crashed near the summit of Crownarad Mountain above Fintra,

north-west of Killybegs, in the Irish Republic. The aircraft
disintegrated. When rescuers reached the site three hours later,
the wreckage was still burning. Members of the Ordinance
Corps dealt with two unexploded depth charges and hundreds
of rounds of machine-gun bullets. It fell to the Irish Army
Medical Service to recover the remains, which were placed in
coffins and assigned death certificates.

Seventy years after the accident, I hiked to the crash site
where engines and fragments still lie. Climbing high over
Donegal Bay, I knew this was an experience for which nothing
could prepare me. Members of other families had flown from
Australia and Scotland. We were joined by more than eighty
local people. One by one, schoolchildren read out the names of
the crewmen.

We learnt that, in the intervening years, residents living in the
shadow of the mountain, as well as others over the border in
Northern Ireland, had gone there to remember and pray for
twelve people they had never met. As I stood in the cold mountain air and untied the RAF coastal command flag covering the
memorial, I was moved by the selfless generosity of strangers
who described these young men as their unknown 'brothers in
faith'. Two generations on, they upheld us in our emotional
remembrance, becoming the presence of God for us that day.

9

Bridges

The city of Bruges near the coast of Belgium is renowned for its striking churches, convents and *Godshuizen*, houses of God hidden away behind walls and grouped around neat courtyard gardens. The 'Venice of the North' is also famed for its meandering canals and pathways over them – which is hardly surprising, for Bruges (or *Brugge*) means 'bridges'.

One cold January day, I found myself ambling along those winding streets. My friend was recovering from his depression and we had decided that a trip to Belgium by Eurostar would be a complementary therapy in the dark of winter. After legging it around museums and peering in shops laden with bargain carousels, we made a right turn and were soon crossing a large arched bridge and moving into another world of tall bare poplars and white-facaded houses. We had discovered the Beguinage of the Vineyard (*Begijnhof Ten Wijngaarde*), founded in the thirteenth century during the reign of Margaret of Constantinople.

The Beguines were a movement of lay women contemplatives in northern Europe, whose very presence challenged ecclesiastical and secular forces of medieval society. They aroused suspicion and hatred as well as accusations of heresy because they were deemed to be dangerous free spirits. Some were even burned at the stake, while others took refuge in the cloistered life. But the message of the Beguines was simply to love God, our neighbour and ourselves. They inspire us to have the courage to be ourselves – to share our stories and proclaim the uniqueness of our callings as we follow the way of love. At the Beguinage, we were handed a white card on which were printed words to guide any contemplative in the world:

> Those who enter my house
> should never mention the faults of others.
> Those who gossip
> and do not speak the truth about others
> should stay out of my house.
> Everybody has his faults
> and he should not, therefore, talk
> about those of his fellowmen,
> but consider his own
> and let others be as they are.
> If we are full of love,
> we shall not pay any attention to the faults
> and trespasses of our neighbour.
> If you want to please God and men,
> help to carry your fellowman's burden.
> If you want to avoid sin,
> mind what you say.
>
> If you want real peace,
> look for silence and unity,
> and first try to find out
> about yourself in solitude.
> If ever you get to know bad news,
> ask God to spare you.
> Accept your life
> without questioning the ultimate purpose of God.

There was no single style or pattern of Beguine life. In the early days, most of the women were scattered in different parts of a town or city, coming together daily at particular churches or chapels for Mass. In the Low Countries, such as Belgium, Beguines were often granted land on which to build their own communities and were, in a sense, bridges between the lay and religious worlds. They lived peaceful lives and originally earned their living with looms. They did not take vows but followed strict precepts under the direction of a mistress who guarded the independence of the Beguinage. Despite their lack of a common rule or residence, the unregulated nature of the Beguines' life tended not to meet with clerical approbation and, like many pioneering spirits, they suffered a great deal.

Later, a community of Benedictine sisters was established at the Beguinage in Bruges to continue the tradition of contemplative living. There, at the monastery door, we met a sister who had entered the order when she was twenty-five. 'I am eighty this year and then I can go,' she smiled. A serene and joyful person, she had been educated, I discovered, in the same county as me, and had even been to the cathedral where I had been made a deacon. After speaking about the vocation of 'spreading holiness' in the world, which is very much the heart of becoming the divine presence for others, she took us into a private chapel and invited us to pray with her before the Blessed Sacrament: 'This is a place where you can pray. I find it easy here.' She was right. It was a moment out of time. But as we sunk into the silence, the nun's mobile phone started ringing with a cool tune and, much to her amused embarrassment, she had to fish it out from a pocket in her habit to answer the call from a fellow monastic. Spirituality and humanity are never far apart in the contemplative life. Humour bridges them.

I came to realise in Bruges that, if we are to become the presence of God in the world, we have to offer ourselves as bridges. But bridges can be uncomfortable places because people walk over them. They also need forms of support. The secrets of our calling are often much nearer to us than we know. We go on searching but sometimes they are staring us in the face – literally. My surname, Ford, means a dweller by or at the ford, a shallow area in a river that can be crossed. To ford means to cross over a shallow area.

Months after the visit to Bruges, I was rereading my journals and reminding myself what my spiritual accompanier, a nun in a religious order, had said to me several years ago about my dual place in Anglicanism and Roman Catholicism: 'Your vocation is both traditions – to be a bridge. When I think of your essence it is free spirit.' For over thirty years, I had tried to live out of that vision, galvanised by the vision of Brother Roger, who had discovered his identity as a Christian by reconciling within himself the faith of his spiritual origins and the mystery of the Catholic faith. He felt that if believers could make the unity of Christ's body their 'passionate concern', many connecting roads would be built.

Cyprian Consiglio, the Camaldolese monk and musician who has united West and East in his spiritual practice, goes further: in his understanding of contemplation as a call to everyone, he speaks of universal wisdom as being the bridge between different religions. 'There is such a sense of relief when people who have left Christianity for another contemplative tradition discover not only that Christianity has its own mystical tradition and its own mystical understanding of the Gospel but also that they can integrate into their Christianity the treasure they have found in the other tradition.' Pointing out that bridges go two ways, he continues: 'They not only can help us understand someone else's tradition in a new light; they may also be able to help those from another tradition understand Christianity in a new light as they find in the Christian tradition resonances of their own spiritual theology.'[1]

Our calling to become the presence of God, then, can cross denominational lines as well as boundaries of faith. This came home to me once in the French town of Grenoble where I witnessed a young man crash his motorcycle near a tram station. Thinking he was dead, I ran over to discover him very much alive. Nonetheless, with cuts on his body, he was dazed and in pain. His main concern seemed to be the welfare of his bike. As he tried to move it, others came to help. Then, as we waited for an ambulance, a woman poured water from a plastic bottle over his stomach wound. He winced. Even in his discomfort, he thanked me for waiting, although I had done nothing except pick up his lighter. 'Thank God for your life,' I replied in French. He smiled and waved his arms heavenwards: 'Thanks be to Allah.' Only then did I learn he was a Muslim.

The Rebuilding of a Broken Vessel

Corporate banker Dara Westby lives in a small fishing port on the east coast of Ireland. For many years, he held a senior position with a financial institution and travelled the globe. His career was heading in the right direction. Then, in what many saw as a reckless gamble, he decided to take time out – not to lounge around or play golf all day, but to explore the depths of his inner life by studying for a master's degree in Christian Spirituality and training to be a spiritual director.

A separated man, Dara has returned to his home town of Skerries (which means 'The Rocks') to bring up his young daughter, Megan. He attends Mass each day, is a member of the local parish pastoral council and volunteers with the St Vincent de Paul Society, an organisation dedicated to tackling poverty and supporting the marginalised. As he brings the presence of God to others, he bridges many different worlds.

'I believe that our DNA is programmed to some degree to be monastic,' he told me. 'My home is my monastic cell in a modern world, a place where I can become attentive to the presence, action and the movements of God in my ordinary human experiences. I listen to Zen music in the house and have a Zen bell on my mobile phone. It is a place where I can take a long, loving look at the Real. Here I can sift through the reality of life: feelings, inclinations, attractions, choices made or avoidance of choices, moments of consolation or times of desolation. I'm seeking to identify what aligns me to God and what pulls me away from God.

'We are not so much human beings on a spiritual journey as spiritual beings on a human journey. Unfortunately, I think there is a tendency to view this human journey in isolation from what has come before and what is ahead of us in eternity.'

Both sides of Dara's family have a rich Roman Catholic heritage. His uncle, Gerry, is a Franciscan missionary priest in Latin America. His mother, Maura, is involved in various church ministries as well as a local charismatic prayer group. While grounded in Catholicism and a member of the Emmaus Community, his father, Garry, was part of the Yoga Movement in Ireland during the 1970s. Dara smiles as he recalls those days when Indian visitors would turn up to stay at their house in the Catholic fishing village wearing their saffron robes and prayer beads.

Dara's early exposure to the disciplines of meditation and relaxation influenced his later love of the mystical and aesthetic. He also came to respect and honour periods of silence that always took place after their guests from the East had arrived. 'It is in such times that the Holy Spirit can be most at work,' he says. 'Silence is the home of the Word, giving it strength and fruitfulness. Silence is the mystery of the future world. It makes us pilgrims and teaches us to guard the fire within. Silence can be a resting place where God's Spirit whispers to our soul.'

Serving as an altar boy during childhood, Dara grew in his appreciation of the reverence of the Mass and the mystical tradition of Latin benediction. But he also witnessed the raw reality of life as well, and still remembers serving at a funeral where the grief of a young boy became etched in his memory. 'From an early age, I became attuned to the spiritual life. While not having a lexicon to support these inner stirrings, I knew deep within that life was a gift and contained a message and meaning for each one of us,' he told me.

Dara has never forgotten a dreary Thursday at school when he was seventeen which led to a life-changing moment. The nun who usually taught the civics class could not make it, so another teacher wheeled in a television screen and inserted a tape in the video player. By way of introduction, she gave a short talk about a small Yugoslavian village, then groaning under a Communist dictatorship. It was called Medjugorje (meaning 'between the mountains') and since 1981 had witnessed apparitions of the Virgin Mary, who had appeared to six local Catholics. The video met with scepticism and impassiveness from the class. But at least one student responded differently. 'Within a very short period of time,' Dara recalled, 'a feeling enveloped me, something that to this day I cannot explain. It was an absolute conviction in the truth of this story, unlike anything I had experienced before. I had a sense of joy, peace and affirmation that one day I would visit this place in Yugoslavia, a place then I could not even identify on a map.'

During the lunch break, Dara rushed home to share the experience with his mother. She listened with curiosity, but then her two other children arrived back with the news of the day and needed feeding. The subject never arose again between them; yet the teenage Dara was left puzzling over why the Mother of God was apparently visiting earth and there were no television crews covering such a sensational news event.

Then one night, a decade later – when Dara had just turned twenty-seven and was working as an operations manager for an insurance company in Dublin's International Financial Service Centre – he received a call from his mother to tell him that his father had been taken ill. He arranged to meet his mother at the hospital. By morning, Dara's father was still clearly unwell and an exploratory operation was swiftly arranged. Maura Westby immediately got a prayer chain underway through all her friends and prayer group contacts.

Eight hours passed without news. They suspected something was wrong. Later they learned the surgeon had removed a blockage and sent it for analysis. The following morning the consultant summoned the family to his office. He looked uncertain and without much delay said: 'I am sorry to have to tell you but it's cancer.' Like many families in such a situation, the world stopped for a while.

That day Dara and his mother walked Bull Island beach on the shore of Dublin Bay trying to absorb everything. There they comforted each other and composed themselves for the task in hand – breaking the news to a husband and father. Garry Westby had not been informed about the cancer and needed a second operation at another hospital as soon as possible.

'I remember the sunshine on my face, the sound of the crashing waves, the gentle breeze, the screeching of the gulls overhead, the sound of the ferry coming into port,' Dara recollected. 'Life was continuing as normal all around us but how could this be? Had they not heard our news? Within an instant, that sense of conviction, peace, affirmation that I had experienced in the classroom, almost ten years earlier, returned to me. I *would* visit this place called Medjugorje. And Our Lady, who was known in Medjugorje as "Gospa", would help us. After the fall of communism, the town was now in the Herzegovina region of Bosnia and Herzegovina.

'I shared this with Mom and we both recalled my experience in the classroom with a sense of awe and hope. We gave each other a hug, committed to honouring this as soon as we could. Dad underwent his second operation about eight weeks later. This time they cut him open right across his stomach. Now he literally carried a cross on this chest, having previously been cut vertically from the centre of his rib cage down to his naval. The operation lasted nine hours and the surgeon looked shattered. I never prayed so hard for someone I had never met before. I was so glad to see him and so grateful to God for the skill of this man.

'I recall sitting by Dad's bedside shortly after the surgery. He was unconscious and hooked up to a life-support machine for a number of days. His hands – and body – were very cold and recuperation was very slow. There he lay lifeless and yet, beyond the surface, I sensed his spirit resting. I recall quietly praying into his ear. I knew I could be heard. I detected a strange sense of peace in the room, as if someone else was there. But there was no one. A heightened sense of awareness came over me. As Dad's spirit was ever present, so was God's.

'Seven months later, in June 2001, he was fit enough to travel to Medjugorje but he had to stand on the plane for three hours and for a further three-and-a-half hours on the bus – both ways. He could not sit for any length of time because of the scar tissue.

'Although the longer-term prognosis isn't good, our miracle continues thirteen years later. Dad lives month to month in defiance of science as he enjoys his seven grandchildren. His life remains both a gift and a lesson to us all to embrace the present moment.'

For Dara, God is not a distant figure who authored creation at a point in time and sits far off on a chair of judgement, but a deeply personable and intimate lover who longs to be in relationship with each of us. Dara sees God as reaching out to us through the Spirit in the messy and often conflicted situations of everyday life. The fruit of contemplative practice, he believes, is the gentle attentiveness to an extraordinary God in the ordinary circumstances of our daily lives.

But sometimes, Dara believes, it is important to go the extra mile – literally. Prayer is not confined to the comfort of a home or stillness of a church. When his then wife was expecting their daughter, Dara went on a pilgrimage for the safe delivery of the child. In his bare feet, he and a family friend climbed a mountain during the hottest time of day as an offering to God.

'If God willed it, I said I would assume as much pain as possible on the climb as a substitute for my wife feeling pain during the birth,' he explained. 'It was thirty-six degrees centigrade when we commenced our climb. We were both in our bare feet and the stones were like fire. We climbed for over two hours. I was in pain and physically exhausted. I was actually shaking with the fatigue; but I knew deep within that my prayer had been heard. I returned home with a great sense of peace.'

Dara's sister, Karen, is a midwife. She wrote to the hospital for permission to deliver the child. But she was advised that this could only happen if she were scheduled to work that day. Megan was due to be born on the last night of Karen's week of night duty. That evening Dara's wife began to go into labour. When she arrived at the hospital, she was the only pregnant woman admitted that night to the maternity ward and Karen was there to welcome the couple. Megan was brought into the world by Karen forty minutes later.

'Very shortly after, I was left for a brief period in the silence of the night, holding our new daughter in my arms,' said Dara. 'I thanked God for this miracle of new life: my prayers had been answered. However, due to circumstances beyond my control, our marriage broke up three years later. I was in much pain at the loss of the relationship and all the broken dreams. We had been together since our early twenties. I was deeply aware of the instability this produced in Megan's life and unsure of the path to take. So eventually I set off on another pilgrimage to Medjugorje for a time of quiet prayer and reflection. By now, I had been there several times. I had been adjusting to the new circumstances of my life: being the primary carer for Megan, holding down a full-time job and trying to study. There had been little time to reflect on these new circumstances of my life; so many questions remained unanswered.

'Arriving in Medjugorje with my parents and Megan, I came to a deeper awareness of my own inner brokenness. That evening we went to the adoration service. For the first time, I was not there out of deep gratitude for my life circumstances, but instead bearing much despair. My mother knelt quietly beside me in prayer, carrying pain for a son as only a mother can. I cried out to God from the very depths of my being just like the psalmist: "My soul cries out to you oh Lord – Oh Lord, hear my voice."

'Surrounded by many other pilgrims, I pleaded with God from the depths of my heart for a sign that would allow me to know what path to take. The reflective music stopped. There was silence for a few minutes as we knelt in the night air, surrounded by the sound of crickets, and prayed in front of the Blessed Sacrament. Then the priest, quoting from Isaiah 49, began a meditation that seemed to speak to me personally. I broke down in tears and was in awe. I felt my mother shudder beside me and then realised that she, too, was crying quietly. In the depths of my brokenness, God had communicated to me in a powerful way. God was in all of this and would not forget me.'

Despite the worries assailing Dara, there were to be further indications that God had not abandoned him. He happened to come across a book, *Can You Drink The Cup?* by Henri Nouwen, which challenged him to go deeper and led him on a new spiritual quest.[2] It would eventually culminate in his taking a sabbatical from the world of global finance and entering the halls of academia. Nonetheless, it remained a bleak time in Dara's life with many unanswered questions. The global economy – and Ireland's 'Celtic Tiger' – had just crashed and, with it, 'the decadent consumerism of postmodern Ireland that had engulfed our country during that time'.

As Dara was working at the cutting edge of the financial services industry, he was witnessing first-hand the extent of the fall. The economy of Ireland had seen a period of rapid economic growth between 1995 and 2000, fuelled by foreign direct investment and a subsequent property price bubble which made the real economy uncompetitive.

In addition, the separation from his wife was causing an acute spiritual pain. In his lonely new role as a single parent to a little girl, his inner journey in search of meaning intensified. He told me that Nouwen's writings had begun to speak to him in the silence – and sometimes turmoil – of the night. The words were direct, lucid and heartfelt. 'It was as though Nouwen himself was present in the room speaking with me, not so much from a position of authority, but as a fellow seeker who had also experienced the anguish and pain of life's journey. The self-implicating nature of Nouwen's writing provided a lantern at that time.

'Thanks to Nouwen's works, I came to realise that I was standing in the darkness. I couldn't see the way ahead but I was holding a lantern with enough light to take one step forward.

'Nouwen challenged me to explore my own Christian identity further: to recognise and break open those words "beloved son" and to live more authentically, seeing my brokenness as a blessing to be shared with others.'

Another invaluable roadmap was the practice of spiritual direction where one person is present with another, attentive to the work of the Spirit in that individual's life, relationships, work and prayers, and where both can listen and discern. This helped Dara connect his own private prayer life with the wider community and world. 'It has become a bridge for me between religion and spirituality – where my own critical interiority meets my faith tradition,' he said. 'In early Celtic spirituality, the *anam cara* (soul friend) was a person who acted as companion or spiritual guide. This relationship was considered sacred and went beyond the normal confines of friendship. To the *anam cara* you could expose your true self, your innermost self, your mind and heart. You were joined in an ancient and eternal way to the friend of your soul. You were understood without any superficiality. This was considered God's gift where you felt the shelter of another's soul.

'I believe that in everyone's life there is a great need for an *anam cara*. It's about going to the wilderness of the soul with another but not so much about finding the way out. It's about meeting the person where they are, respecting the disorder and confusion, but not about imposing an order of logic. It's about being present to another person's pain but not taking their pain away. It's about bearing witness to the struggles of others but not about directing those struggles. It's about listening with the heart, not analysing in the head.

'I am blessed to have such an *anam cara* in my life: someone forty years my senior with very different life experience. A woman in a religious order, she is Kathleen O'Brien (Sister of Marie Reparatrice) and lives in a community 200 miles away. At one level it might seem we have nothing in common, yet I have never known a friendship like it. We carry each other, are there for each other and support each other with the absolute conviction that we are bound beyond the parameters of space and time by the Creator Spirit. I thank God that I walk this journey in the presence of my *anam cara*. It is a reminder that we do not journey alone but listen together to those words we so often hear in scripture: *Do not be afraid.*

'To become the presence of God for others in the world or to become spiritually present is to recognise the precious gift of the present moment. There are two days in the year we cannot control: yesterday because it has passed and tomorrow because it has not arrived.'

Dara, who completed his course in spiritual direction with the Vincentians, believes that, in its simplest form, prayer is about thinking and living in the presence of God. In prayer, people discover who they truly are, intensifying what it means to be alive in the world. It is an endless dialogue between the creator and the creation. Prayer is not something among other things that we simply *do*, but should become the underlying receptive attitude out of which all life can receive new vitality.

Real prayer pulls us away from our own self-preoccupations, encourages us to leave familiar ground and challenges us to enter into a new world that cannot be contained within the narrow boundaries of our minds and hearts.

Prayer also entails surrender. It is about letting go. It is the way to let the life-giving Spirit of God penetrate the deep crevices of our being. Prayer is where we meet our own finiteness against the infinite and omnipotent power of God. It is honouring the power of silence and recognising that it is pregnant with possibility. It allows us to enter the great cloud of unknowing. Prayer is a way of life which allows us to find stillness in the midst of turmoil. It offers the opportunity for spiritual growth and sometimes provides a glimpse of the great mysterious light behind the curtain of life, the God who is always new, always different.

Dara's spiritual practice is focused on Centering Prayer, a movement co-founded by the Cistercian monk, Father Thomas Keating. It is a method which facilitates the development of contemplative prayer and empowers people to perceive, relate to and respond with increasing sensitivity to the divine presence and action in, through, and beyond everything that exists.

According to Father Keating, Centering Prayer is like two friends sitting in silence, being in each other's presence. For Dara, the practice has become the bridge between his conscious and unconscious life. He says it helps him move beyond the psychic level of rational thinking and logical understanding into the transpersonal realm, going beyond thoughts and emotions and into the Great Silence: 'Be still and know that I am God; Be still and know that I am; Be still and know; Be still; Be.'

Prayer also infuses Dara's daily encounter with God through the Mass. He explains that, through the eucharist, he transcends the boundaries of time and joins the apostles at the Last Supper: 'Here I truly immerse myself in those words "Give us this day our daily bread". Here I consecrate my life to the Lord through the Holy Sacrifice at the altar. I present my plans for the day to the Lord and ask him to bless them. Here I offer petitions for those I carry in my heart and those who cry out to the Lord in expectant faith.'

To be spiritually present, says Dara, is to recognise the truth of a prayer by the sixteenth-century mystic St Teresa of Avila:

> Christ has no body but yours,
> No hands, no feet on earth but yours,
> Yours are the eyes with which he looks
> Compassion on this world
> Yours are the feet with which he walks to do good
> Yours are the hands, with which he blesses all the world.
> Yours are the hands, Yours are the feet,
> Yours are the eyes, you are his body.
> Christ has no body now but yours,
> No hands, no feet on earth but yours,
> Yours are the eyes with which he looks
> Compassion on this world.
> Christ has no body on earth now but yours.

Early in 2009, ahead of a court hearing in connection with his marriage, Dara needed time away and felt prompted to visit the Marian shrine of Knock in County Mayo. He hadn't been there for many years and on this occasion his mother joined him. The spiritual significance of Knock began one August evening in 1879 when the Virgin Mary, St Joseph and St John the Evangelist are believed to have appeared at the south gable of the village church. Beside them and to their left was an altar with a cross and the figure of a lamb, around which angels were reported to hover. There were fifteen official witnesses to the apparition who watched and prayed for two hours in the teeming rain. Two commissions of enquiry – in 1879 and 1936 – accepted their testimony as trustworthy and satisfactory.

Knock made a profound impression on Dara and Maura, especially after they discovered the prayer centre which offered guided reflections throughout the day. 'This is how God brought me from the depths of brokenness and spoke to me through the silent contemplation of guided reflection,' said Dara.

The first guided reflection was on *The Wedding Feast of Cana* (Jn 2). Dara and Maura entered the room, which was decorated beautifully with art and had a candle burning. Quiet, reflective music was playing. About fifteen people were already there. They glanced at each other, acknowledging that the theme was not merely coincidental. They believed God was working there and setting the scene.

'I reflected on the reason why I was there – a failed marriage,' said Dara. 'When I heard Mary's words of obedience from that chapter – "Do whatever he tells you" – they penetrated with such depth. I was grieving our loss. Here I was observing the old ceremonial jars of water from the Old Testament being enriched into the New Testament wine; here I found myself – a ceremonial jar waiting to be transformed – re-invigorated and filled anew.'

The second reflection later that day was *The Road to Emmaus* (Lk 24:13). Again Dara reflected on its poignancy and applied it to his own situation. 'Here were Mom and I, two disciples on the road, discussing what had happened, its meaning and consequences, and questioning why things had turned out as they had. It was only when the reflection had come to an end that I realised Mom and I were the only two pilgrims in the room, just like the two disciples on the road. Our hearts also burned.'

That evening the third reflection was on *The Washing of the Feet* (Jn 13). About twenty people were present. Dara and Maura say they felt the presence of the Holy Spirit. The art had changed, as had the music. But the flame of the candle still flickered.

'I reflected on this scripture passage and how it resonated with my circumstances. Marriage was about serving the other with *loyalty* and *obedience*, in *vulnerability* and *eternally*. That's what love stood for. I had entered into the depth of mystery that such vows held. I had always been very caring and generous. Mom confirmed that all the family had worried about me throughout my relationship as they observed it from the sides. Yet I had fallen in love with this person so many years ago. She had touched my heart. Had this not been of God?

'Later that evening we went to Mass. The sermon was based on Matthew 10:26: "Do not be afraid." Somehow everything was connecting. I was filled with great mystery and awe.

'We then went for dinner in the hotel attached to the shrine. We sat and shared about the richness of the day. I looked across the room and saw a woman sitting on her own. I recalled the many times of international travelling in my work as a banker when I had felt awkward and lonely, having to sit in busy restaurants on my own. I asked Mom if she would mind if this person joined us. She turned out to be from Cork and a mother of four. She had made the journey by public transport on her own to spend a few days at the shrine.

'We had a great conversation over the meal and then talked about books. The pilgrim asked me who my favourite author was. I said that in recent times I had been particularly drawn to Henri Nouwen, and that I had just finished a book called *Can You Drink the Cup*? in which the author reflects on Jesus lifting the cup of wine at the Last Supper and offering a prayer. Shortly afterwards, a waiter arrived and placed a glass of red wine on the table beside me. We looked at each other puzzled – no one had ordered it.

'I gently called the waiter back. He bent down and confirmed that a monsignor, who had been in the restaurant earlier, had left an instruction for a glass of wine to be brought to me. How could he have known what we would be talking about that evening? We were awestruck, so I decided to order two more glasses and we sat there filled with wonder at what happened – toasting Henri – toasting a mighty God!'

The following day Dara and Maura returned to the prayer centre for more guided reflection and meditation. The first was on Jesus as *The Bread of Life* (Jn 6:22). Dara considered his spiritual development as he identified with the words: 'But don't be concerned about perishable things like food. Spend your energy seeking the eternal life that I, the Son of Man can give you.' He recalled how content he had become over the years, growing in Christ with a joy many others recognised and commented on.

The next reflection was based on *The Storm in the Boat* (Lk 8:22) where Jesus asks his disciples: 'Where is your faith?' Dara made a connection here with the storms in all people's lives, with their noise, aggression, fear and destruction. 'The centre, the eye of the storm, is a place of great silence and peace. Jesus was the eye in my storm and I needed to claim him,' he said.

The Potter (Jer 18) was the focus of the third reflection. Dara went on: 'It has that image of God gently moulding the clay in his hands in such a delicate, patient, loving way. Here I was before God, a broken vessel lacking definition. But God in his love and mercy could take this offering of material and mould me back to a new creation with a new purpose. What wonderful words of comfort to be left with. I was in God's hands and he would form me anew.'

As the years passed, Dara's life slowly changed from one of brokenness to one of blessing. A fractured vessel was gradually rebuilt, culminating in triumphant academic success and a qualification as a spiritual director so that he can spread holiness and become the presence of God to others in a more con-templative way. The wounds, of course, emerge from time to time, but there has also been healing and grace. On the shores of the small Irish fishing village, Dara reflects: 'While unsure of my route at times, the Divine Navigator gently directed my course out of the rough waters and into the safety of port where the necessary maintenance could be performed, supplies attained and a welcome rest secured. Now I stand on the dock refreshed, gazing out on the waters, ready to cast my sails and wondering where the boat's course will take me.'

Meanwhile, Dara's daughter, whom he has protected throughout the painful years of separation, remains at the heart of his spiritual care. Faithfully, at the end of each day, Dara prays with Megan, then draws from *The Rivers of Life*, a Vincentian contemplation tool and a form of *examen*. There are four rivers to be negotiated in this exercise: *The River of Inspiration*: What inspired me today? Where did I see God? *The River of Joy*: What brought me joy today and where did I see God? *The River of Challenge*: What challenged me today and what is God saying to me? *The River of Sadness*: What made me sad today and what is God saying to me?'

'It really is', adds Dara, 'a wonderful and precious time for both of us. In the silence of the night, we are gently reminded that we are all interconnected, interrelated and part of God's ongoing plan. We are stitched together like pieces of a patchwork quilt and, in difficult times, God rebuilds his broken vessels with care. It is all a gift – it is all God's grace.'

Postscript

One afternoon, after I had stepped back from ordained life and was contemplating the future in a fog of confusion, a young pigeon collapsed under a bush after being mauled by a cat. It appeared as if it might die. As I knelt over the poor creature, it appeared to symbolise the state of my vocation. But instead of taking the bird to the vet, who would have put it to sleep, I quietly stayed with the pigeon. In the name of Christ, I laid my hands over its body and prayed. Within minutes, the pigeon began to walk again, though it was clearly bewildered. Over the ensuing days, I nurtured the bird with seed and water before taking it to a natural habitat. The recovery was gradual but I did not give up hope. Eventually, the pigeon regained its strength by taking its time. Then, suddenly one morning, the bird flew off to become itself again.

It was a difficult couple of years as I readjusted to a new way of being, but I always kept the pigeon's recovery in mind, as it seemed to denote the trust in God I needed to see me through. It also signified the freedom that ministering on the margins could mean. These days, I often find myself trying to help people whose faith is not robust but who still believe 'in something' – or people whose faith *is* strong but who feel alienated for whatever reason from institutional Christianity. There is no doubt in my mind that I am called to the edge and that ministry just happens.

I remember meeting a nun who had worked with refugees and people living with HIV and AIDS. She had discovered on the margins people who had called forth something in her of love and compassion because of the love and compassion they showed each other. Refugees had so little, yet always shared what they had with someone who had even less. 'I think Christ is actually not on the edges but in the centre, although he is not always acknowledged there,' she told me. 'As institutionalised human beings, we begin to see the world in a much narrower way than he sees it. Christ will not allow himself to be excluded so he is at the centre of an institution. I need to have links with an institution but I need to do that with the vision of Christ at the edges.'

In their book, *Urgings of the Heart*, Wilkie Au and Noreen Cannon remind us that all ministry should focus on God, not us. We are ministers only because 'God has cut us in on the action'. The authors continue: 'God invites us to give human form to the divine presence and love that abound in every nook and cranny of creation. We are called to be, in the words of Ignatius, "contemplatives even in action", people who have a facility for finding God in all things.'[1] This is similar to what the Jesuit writer Karl Rahner speaks about in *The Mystical Way in Everyday Life*. He points out that the 'simple and honestly accepted everyday life contains in itself the eternal and the silent mystery, which we call God and his secret grace, especially when this life remains the everyday'.[2]

Through the writers I have quoted, the people I have interviewed and the pilgrimage I have drawn from, I hope you might be inspired to become a more compassionate minister to your neighbour, a light in the dark world of which we are part. We can all make mistakes and our judgements may not always be balanced; but a spirit of service after the self-emptying pattern of Christ, rather than any inclination towards any form of spiritual power, is a prerequisite. Somehow, my ordination still holds significance and, as an ecumenist, it seems appropriate to have been made a deacon 'in the church of God'. But not everything in life is explainable and our stories are always part of the divine mystery. Ordination might not only be about the future; it might also signify something about the past.

There is so much need in the world and each of us has to learn *our* way of responding spiritually to it. I began with correspondence from a former monk who moved from seeking God on his knees as a Trappist to becoming the presence of God on his feet as a postman. He reminded us that swift and simple solutions are not the usual course of the spiritual life. It is in the faithful, daily struggle that our identity in Christ takes shape. Robert Durback followed the path of his unique journey and we can only pursue ours in our own direction. At the end of the day, we have to work out *for ourselves* how we bring this presence to others, for each of us is different. There cannot be templates as such because every situation is distinctive. But we must not be in it *for ourselves*.

Thomas Merton reminds us that we do not exist for ourselves alone. Only when we are completely convinced of this can we begin to love ourselves as we should – and this naturally involves loving others too. For Merton, loving ourselves correctly means primarily desiring to *live*: accepting life as 'a very great gift and a great good, not because of what it gives us, but because of what it enables us to give to others.'[3]

Giving human form to the divine presence will always require humility and it may sometimes result in humiliation. This, though, is the way of Christ and an invitation for each us to grow more deeply and genuinely into the ways of God. But any service in the name of the divine has to be contemplative rather than clericalised, flowering from a compassionate heart and not a controlling temperament.

Desideratum

to live not as one
who knows but as one
who wonders

to exist not as one
who is but as one
who yearns to be

to journey not as one
who leads but as one
who seeks

to speak not as one
who answers but as one
who questions

to touch not as one
who possesses but as one
who cherishes

to hope not as one
who awaits but as one
who creates

to relate not as one
who controls but as one
who empowers

to pray not as one
who recites but as one
who overflows

Sister Kathleen Waters OCSO,
Trappistine Abbey of Notre-Dame de l'Assomption
Rogersville, New Brunswick, Canada

My interior life is a walk through darkness with the God within who leads us beyond and out of ourselves to become a vessel of Divine Love let loose upon the world.

Sister Joan Chittister, OSB

Notes

Introducing … The Monk and The Postman

1 Brother David Steindl-Rast in William Elliott, *Tying Rocks to Clouds: Meetings and Conversations with Wise and Spiritual People*. New York, Image (Doubleday), 1996, p. 246.

1. Being Ourselves

1 Mark Barrett, *Crossing: Reclaiming the Landscape of our Lives*. London, Darton, Longman and Todd, 2001, p. 11.
2 St Ambrose on Psalm 118, from *The Glenstal Book of Prayer*. Dublin, The Columba Press, 2001, p. 64.
3 From a BBC Radio 4 Lent course, *Were You There?*, broadcast in 1994.
4 *The Way of a Pilgrim*, unattributed, translated from the Russian by R.M. French. London, Triangle, 1995, p. 1.
5 *The Glenstal Book of Prayer*, op. cit.
6 Karl Rahner, SJ, *The Mystical Way in Everyday Life*. New York, Orbis Books, 2011, p. 159.
7 Henri J.M. Nouwen, *The Inner Voice of Love: A Journey Through Anguish to Freedom*. New York, Doubleday, 1996, p. 67.
8 David Steindl-Rast, OSB, with Sharon Lebell, *The Music of Silence: Entering the Sacred Space of Monastic Experience*. San Francisco: HarperSanFrancisco, 1995.
9 Ibid. p. 5.
10 Ibid. p. 17.
11 Ibid. p. 18.
12 Ibid. p. 12.
13 *Cold Mountain* (director, Anthony Minghella), 2003.

[14] *Breaking and Entering* (director, Anthony Minghella), 2006.

[15] Thomas Merton, *No Man is an Island*. London, Burns and Oates, 1985, p. xxi.

2. The Madness of Love

[1] William Paulsell, *Letters from a Hermit*. Springfield, Templegate Publishers, 1978, p. 97.

[2] Ibid. p. 98.

[3] Op. cit.

[4] Ibid. p. 95.

[5] Ibid. pp. 101–2.

[6] Ibid. pp. 116–7.

[7] Matthew Kelty, *Sermons in a Monastery*. Kalamazoo, Cistercian Publications, 1983, p. 35.

[8] Ibid. p. 38.

[9] Ibid. p. 16.

[10] *The Compline Talks of Father Matthew Kelty*, The Abbey of Gethsemani, CD, 2004.

[11] Kelty, op. cit. p. 30.

[12] Paulsell, op. cit. p. 4.

[13] A Monk, *The Hermitage Within*. London, Darton, Longman and Todd, 1999.

[14] Ibid. Publisher's Foreword.

[15] Ibid. Part One, The Desert, unpaginated.

[16] Ibid.

[17] Ibid. p. 140.

[18] Ibid. p. 141.

[19] From the *Glenstal Bible Missal*. London, Collins Liturgical Publications, 1984, p. 763.

[20] Maggie Ross, *Writing the Icon of The Heart: In Silence Beholding*. Abingdon, The Bible Reading Fellowship, 2011, p. 95.

[21] Wayne Teasdale, *A Monk in the World: Cultivating a Spiritual Life*. Novato, New World Library, 2002, p. xxvi.

3. Hollowed Out

[1] Jean-Marie Howe OCSO, *Secret of the Heart: Spiritual Being*. Kalamazoo, Cistercian Publications, 2005, p. 23.
[2] Rainer Maria Rilke, *Rodin*. London, The Grey Walls Press, 1946, p. 9.
[3] Howe, op. cit. p. 23.
[4] Jean-Marie Howe, *Spiritual Journey: The Monastic Way*. Rogersville, Abbaye Notre-Dame de l'Assomption, 1989, p. 50.
[5] Ibid. p. 10.
[6] Ibid. p. 13.
[7] Ibid. p. 14.
[8] Ibid. p. 15.
[9] Brother Lawrence, *The Practice of the Presence of God*. Oxford, Oneworld Publications, 1993.
[10] Ibid. p. 4.
[11] Ibid. p. 26.
[12] Ibid. p. 39.
[13] Ibid. p. 21.
[14] Ibid. p. 68.
[15] Ibid. p. 59.
[16] Ibid. p. 30.

4. Awakening to Reality

[1] Teasdale, op. cit. p. 8.
[2] Dumitru Staniloae, *Prayer and Holiness*. Oxford, SLG Press, 1996, p. 1.
[3] Teasdale, op. cit. p. 8
[4] Maria Boulding OSB, *Gateway to Hope: An Exploration of Failure*. London, Fount Paperbacks, 1985.

[5] Maria Boulding OSB, *Gateway to Resurrection*. London, Burns & Oates, 2010, p. 4.
[6] Ibid. p. 5.

5. Contemplatives or Clerics?

[1] Henri J.M. Nouwen, *In the Name of Jesus: Reflections on Christian Leadership*. London, Darton, Longman and Todd, 1989, p. 22.
[2] Ibid. pp. 29–30.
[3] Henri J.M. Nouwen, *The Path of Power*. London, Darton, Longman and Todd, 1995.
[4] Ibid. pp. 14–15.
[5] Brian Thorne, *Person-Centred Counselling and Christian Spirituality*. London, Whurr Publications, 1998.
[6] Ibid. p. 11.
[7] Thomas Keating, *Reflections on the Unknowable*. New York, Lantern Books, 2014, p. 56.
[8] Ibid. p. 58.
[9] Teasdale, op. cit. p. xxx.
[10] Ibid. p. 57.
[11] William McNamara, *The Human Experience: A Divine Madness*. Silver Spring, 2010, p. xxvi.
[12] Ibid. p. 133.
[13] Ibid. p. 134.
[14] *Calvary* (director, John Michael McDonagh), 2014.
[15] Maggie Ross, *Pillars of Flame: Power, Priesthood, and Spiritual Maturity*. New York, Church Publishing, 2007.
[16] Ron Seitz, *A Memory Vision of Thomas Merton: Song for Nobody*. Liguori, Triumph Books, 1995, p. 93.
[17] Fr David Mills, *Taunton Catholic Church Magazine*, Christmas 2014.

[18] John O'Donohue, *Minding the Threshold: Towards a Theory of Priesthood in Difficult Times. The Furrow*, vol. 49, no. 6, June 1998, p. 323.
[19] Ibid. pp. 326–7.
[20] Ibid. p. 327.
[21] Ibid. p. 330.
[22] See Howe, *Spiritual Journey*, op. cit. pp. 81–96.
[23] Ibid. p. 92.
[24] Ibid. p. 94.
[25] Ibid. p. 95.

6. The Blessing of Light

[1] *The Glenstal Book of Prayer*, op. cit. p.14 ff.
[2] Gerald G. May, M.D., *Care of Mind, Care of Spirit: A Psychiatrist Explores Spiritual Direction*. New York, HarperCollins, 1992, p. 22.
[3] Teasdale, op. cit. p. 125.
[4] Teasdale, op. cit. p. 135.
[5] *Still Alice* (directors, Richard Glatzer and Wash Westmoreland), 2014.
[6] Lisa Genova, *Still Alice*. London, Simon & Schuster UK, 2015.
[7] *The Nuns' Story*, broadcast on BBC Radio 4 on 26 March 2006. Producer: Phil Pegum.
[8] Eileen Shamy, *A Guide to the Spiritual Dimension of Care for People with Alzheimer's Disease and Related Dementia: More than Body, Brain and Breath*. London, Jessica Kingsley Publishers, 2003, p. 40.

7. Bearers

[1] Brother Roger of Taizé, *The Rule of Taizé*. New York, The Seabury Press; Les Presses de Taizé, 1968.
[2] Brother Roger of Taizé, op. cit. p. 11.

[3] Brother Roger of Taizé, op. cit. p. 19.
[4] Brother Roger of Taizé, *Essential Writings*. New York, Orbis Books; Ateliers et Presses de Taizé, 2006, p. 68.

8. Befrienders

[1] John O'Donohue, *Anam Cara: Spiritual Wisdom from the Celtic World*. London, Bantam Press, 1998, p. 243.
[2] Ibid.
[3] John O'Donohue, op. cit. p. 245.
[4] John O'Donohue, op. cit. p. 246.
[5] John O'Donohue, op. cit. pp. 268–9.
[6] William Elliott, op. cit. p. 248.
[7] Ibid. p. 254.
[8] Ibid. p. 248.

9. Bridges

[1] Cyprian Consiglio, *Prayer in the Cave of the Heart: The Universal Call to Contemplation*. Collegeville, Liturgical Press, 2010, pp. 8–9.
[2] Henri J.M. Nouwen, *Can You Drink The Cup?* Notre Dame, Indiana, Ave Maria Press, 1996.

Postscript

[1] Wilkie Au and Noreen Cannon, *Urgings of the Heart: A Spirituality of Integration*. Mahwah, Paulist Press, 1995, p. 140.
[2] Karl Rahner, SJ, op. cit. p. 173.
[3] Thomas Merton, op. cit. p. xix.

Books By Michael Ford

Wounded Prophet

Father Mychal Judge

Eternal Seasons

Disclosures

Song of the Nightingale

The Dance of Life

Arrivals and Departures

Spiritual Masters for All Seasons

Watershed

Michael Ford's website can be found at
www.hermitagewithin.co.uk